TIME

STAR TREK

Inside the Most Influential Science-Fiction Series Ever

CONTENTS

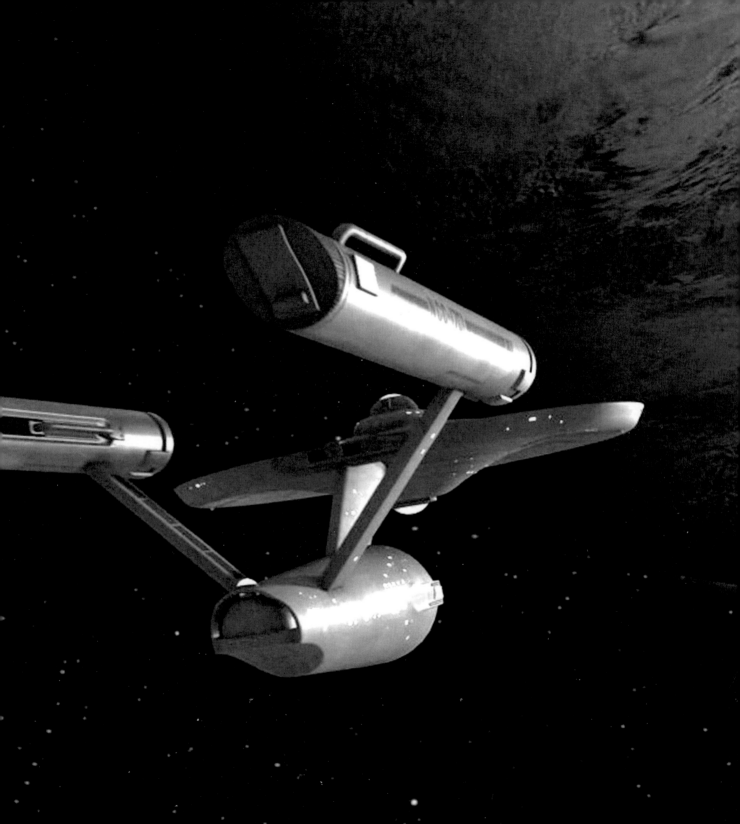

The starship *Enterprise*, the primary setting for the *Star Trek* series, travels through space to explore new worlds and boldly go where none have gone before.

CAPTAIN'S LOG: AN INTRODUCTION

AFTER 50 YEARS, THE TRUTH IS CLEAR: *STAR TREK* IS MORE THAN JUST A TV SHOW. IT'S AN IDEA THAT CHANGED THE WORLD

BY THOMAS E. WEBER

EVERYONE DISCOVERS THE POWER OF STAR TREK IN HIS OR HER OWN WAY.

FOR ME, IT WAS A CHILDHOOD bonding experience with my grandfather, a Scottish immigrant whose brogue had a tendency to become more impenetrable when he was excited—a trait he shared with a certain chief engineer of the U.S.S. *Enterprise*. *Star Trek*'s first run had ended in 1969, but by the early 1970s, the show was beginning to find a robust second life in reruns. My grandfather and I would sit together and watch, thrilled whenever Scotty

had a chance to do more than energize the transporter beam. The more I saw, the more captivating *Trek*'s fictional future seemed. Powerful computers. Constant adventure. And people committed to doing the right thing in the face of complicated moral dilemmas. I was hooked.

So were millions of other fans around the world. *Star Trek*, it turned out, was something much more than a popular television show. As we mark the 50th anniversary of its first episode, the phenomenon that is *Star Trek* is stronger than ever—with a 13th feature film arriving and a new series set to begin streaming in early 2017.

To commemorate this landmark anniversary, TIME's editors examined the big question at the heart of all the passion and devotion: Why is *Star Trek* so influential? As you'll see in this book, the answer is far

more complex than the show's capacity for telling good dramatic stories (though *Trek* has produced plenty of those). No, to really understand *Star Trek*'s appeal, you need to go back to the very beginning, as we do in "A Bold Vision," to look at the DNA that Gene Roddenberry, the TV show's creator, encoded deep in its design. Roddenberry, as you'll see, didn't just want to depict adventures in space. He wanted to show how the future offered the possibility of humans searching for the best in themselves and in one another.

That DNA imbued *Star Trek*'s fictional universe with an uncanny ability to connect with our real one in a number of ways. In "Diversity on the Bridge," you'll learn how the show's forward-thinking casting helped inspire optimism about equal rights for all. "Racing to Space" details the ways *Star Trek* forged

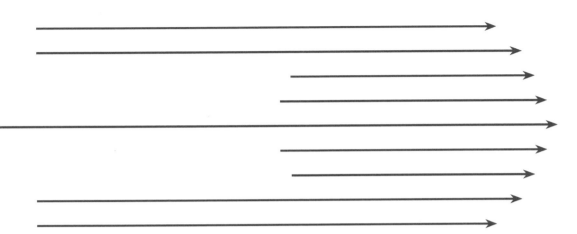

a link with the U.S. space program—right down to a real-life space shuttle named *Enterprise*. "Wait . . . Are They Making That Up?" looks at the theories behind *Trek*'s futuristic science, such as faster-than-light travel. And in "The Future of Gadgets Is Now," we reveal the true stories of how the hardware of Starfleet helped inspired the technology we rely on every day.

Because alien life offered a singularly compelling way to hold a mirror up to humanity, *Star Trek* introduced a long line of memorable extraterrestrials. You can read the stories behind some of the most imaginative aliens in "To Seek Out New Life" and also find out about an actual Klingon war: a legal battle over the fictional race's invented language. In "Spock and Awe," you'll get the inside scoop on the creation of history's most famous Vulcan and his relationship with

Capt. Kirk from none other than William Shatner himself.

In "Rise of the Trekker," we uncover an energy source more powerful than the *Enterprise*'s antimatter engines: Trekkers, the dedicated fans who have kept *Star Trek* at the forefront of pop culture for over five decades. (We also present a completely impartial analysis of which space franchise is superior: *Star Trek* or *Star Wars*.) And in our closing chapter, "A Political Enterprise," you'll gain insight into the politics that have made *Star Trek* uniquely relevant, then and now.

Fifty years. Five TV series. Hundreds of episodes and a galaxy of characters, ships and plots. There's plenty to explore, so read on—and live long and prosper.

Thomas E. Weber is TIME's executive editor.

Weber meets Leonard Nimoy backstage at Detroit's Fisher Theatre in 1976. Nimoy was starring in a stage production of Sherlock Holmes.

A BOLD VISION

AT A TIME WHEN WESTERNS
AND COMEDIES RULED TV,
GENE RODDENBERRY DREAMED UP
A DIFFERENT KIND OF SHOW.
FIFTY YEARS LATER, THAT CONCEPT
IS STILL GOING STRONG

BY RICHARD ZOGLIN

L IKE ONE OF THOSE PRIMITIVE PLANETS THE *ENTERPRISE* CREW
would occasionally stumble upon (and where they would have
to make sure, thanks to the Prime Directive, not to use their futuristic knowledge and gear to alter the civilization's normal course
of development), the birth of *Star Trek* seems now to date from
an almost prehistoric television era. Creator Gene Roddenberry
pitched his space-adventure series to the networks as a "Wagon
Train to the Stars," a nod to the westerns that were still the gold
standard in popular TV drama in the 1960s. The special effects
were almost comically low-tech—all those toy-chest phaser guns,
tin-foil headpieces for the aliens and stock shots of crew members
getting jostled in the corridor whenever an explosion rocked the
ship. (Seatbelts weren't required in cars yet, much less spaceships.)
The *Enterprise* never actually landed on any of the planets it visited—crew members were "beamed" there instead—for the simple
reason that the special effects would have been too costly.

From left: Leonard Nimoy, director Robert
Wise, Gene Roddenberry, DeForest Kelley
and William Shatner on the set of *Star Trek:
The Motion Picture* in 1978.

"Space: the final frontier," intoned William Shatner in the show's famous opening, announcing the U.S.S. *Enterprise*'s five-year mission to explore new worlds, to seek out new civilizations, to "boldly go where no man has gone before." But the mission ended in 1969 after just three seasons, when NBC canceled the series because of low ratings that today, in the fragmented cable world, would have been hailed as a smash success.

Yet *Star Trek* had an unlikely rebirth and journeyed on to become the most durable cult

RODDENBERRY PITCHED HIS SPACE-ADVENTURE SERIES TO THE NETWORKS AS A "WAGON TRAIN TO THE STARS."

hit in TV history. The series got a second wind in syndicated reruns; then came a Saturday-morning cartoon series (with the voices of most of the original cast); then, in 1979, the first of six feature films reuniting the TV crew on the big screen. A sequel to the original series, *Star Trek: The Next Generation*, debuted in 1987 and became the highest-rated series in syndicated (off-network) television. That was followed by three more TV series and six more movies, featuring both the *Next Generation* cast and a new set of actors portraying the original *Enterprise* crew in their younger days. Yet another feature film—the 13th, *Star Trek Beyond*—will hit theaters in July 2016.

The show was a merchandising bonanza, spawning such items as paperback novelizations of *Trek* episodes, T-shirts, action figures, models of the starship *Enterprise*, commemorative coins, video games and *Star Trek* chess sets. The first *Star Trek* convention, held at New York's Statler Hilton hotel in January 1972, drew 3,000 fans; within two years, attendance at the annual get-together had quadrupled. Familiar lines—"Beam me up, Scotty" (which was never actually spoken in precisely those words on the show); "Live long and prosper," Mr. Spock's Vulcan valedictory—became national catchphrases. Enthusiasts wrote books analyzing the show's episodes and ethos; cast members turned out memoirs of their days on the series. The show's futuristic gadgetry anticipated real-life innovations, such as cellphones and medical scanning technology. NASA originally intended to name its first shuttle craft the *Constitution*. After *Trek* fans launched a letter-writing campaign in 1976, the space agency switched to the more popular choice: *Enterprise*.

But *Star Trek* was always more than just a sci-fi nerd's love object. The series was born in the midst of the turbulent 1960s, and its outer-space adventures often reflected and commented on the issues of that divisive decade: the Vietnam War, civil rights, Cold War politics, the budding environmental movement. The show had an idealistic, '60s counterculture mind-set, imagining a 23rd-century world in which humans had outgrown war and prejudice. "We must learn to live together, or most certainly we will soon all die together" was how Roddenberry, who died in 1991, expressed the show's message. "Although *Star Trek* had to entertain or go off the air, we believed our format was unique enough to allow us to challenge and stimulate the audience." *Star Trek* proved that an outer-space action show could appeal to our intelligence, tackle serious issues—and, in a troubled time, offer some hope for the future.

Roddenberry, a Texas-born former Pan Am pilot and press officer for the Los Angeles Police Department, began writing scripts in the 1950s for TV shows like *Dragnet*, *Dr. Kildare* and *Have Gun, Will Travel*. A science-fiction buff since junior high school, he had the idea for a series that would mix the anthology format of sci-fi shows like *The Twilight Zone* and *The Outer Limits* with a cast of continuing characters—a kind of *Gulliver's Travels* of the future, as he once described it.

He took the idea first to program execu-

tives at CBS, who quizzed him for two hours about his plans for the show and then told him goodbye and bought *Lost in Space* instead. He had better luck at NBC, which ordered up a pilot episode. Titled "The Cage," the show starred Jeffrey Hunter (a feature-film star who had appeared with John Wayne in *The Searchers* and played Jesus Christ in *King of Kings*) as a starship captain named Pike who is taken captive on a planet whose inhabitants want to use him to breed a new race. The network rejected the show as "too cerebral" but liked the concept enough to give Roddenberry another chance with a second pilot.

The second go-round featured an almost

From left: Vina (Susan Oliver), Capt. Pike (Jeffrey Hunter) and Number One (Majel Barrett) in the series's original pilot, "The Cage," completed in 1965 and incorporated into the two-part 1966 episode "The Menagerie."

entirely new cast. Replacing Hunter (who decided that starring in a science-fiction series would be a bad career move), Roddenberry cast William Shatner, a Canadian actor with substantial stage and screen experience, as Capt. James T. Kirk. Joining him on the bridge was a conspicuously international crew: a Scottish chief engineer (James Doohan), a Japanese helmsman (George Takei) and an African-American communications chief

(Nichelle Nichols), as well as a nondenominational ship's doctor, played in the pilot by Paul Fix and later by DeForest Kelley.

Only one cast member remained from the original pilot: Leonard Nimoy, as the half-Vulcan, half-human Mr. Spock. NBC wanted to drop him too, complaining that Nimoy's pointy ears and sinister eyebrows made him look "satanic." But Roddenberry insisted on keeping him. "I felt we couldn't do a space show without at least one person on board who constantly reminded you that you are out in space and in a world of the future," he said. "NBC finally agreed to do the second pilot with Spock in it, saying, 'Well, kind of keep him in the background.' " Spock, with his scrupulously logical mind and exotic Vulcan powers, soon became the show's most popular character.

Unlike most TV shows of the day, which could reuse props and sets from other cop shows or westerns or sitcoms, *Star Trek* had to create virtually an entire new world from scratch. The layout of the *Enterprise* was mapped out in detail. Roddenberry obsessed over the verisimilitude of the gadgets, costumes and terminology. Keeping ahead of real-life technology proved to be a challenge. The hand weapons carried by the crew were originally called lasers. When Roddenberry realized that real-life lasers might become commonplace within a few years, he made a last-minute switch and called them "phasers." "We didn't want people saying to us three years from now, 'Oh, come on now, lasers can't do that,' " he explained.

Roddenberry delivered his second pilot in January 1966, and this time NBC picked it up for the fall schedule. *Star Trek* made its network debut on Thursday night, September 8, opposite *My Three Sons* and *Bewitched*. (The first episode was not the pilot but another episode, called "The Man Trap," in which the crew encounter a vampire-like alien that sucks its victims dry of body salt. NBC wanted a monster.) Initial reaction was not encouraging. "*Star Trek* obviously solicits all-out suspension of disbelief, but it won't work," wrote *Variety*. "Even within its sci-fi frame of reference it was an incredible and dreary mess of confusion and complexities."

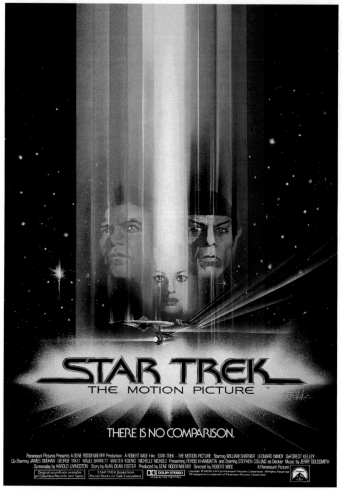

Clockwise from top left: Spock and Kirk debut in the series premiere, airing Sept. 8, 1966; Khan (Ricardo Montalbán) and Joachim (Judson Scott) are antagonists in *Star Trek II: The Wrath of Khan* (1982); Capt. Jean-Luc Picard (Patrick Stewart) and his crew on the bridge in an episode of *The Next Generation* (1988); the official poster for *Star Trek: The Motion Picture* (1979).

Ratings were just good enough to win the series a renewal, but by the middle of its second season, NBC was ready to cancel it. A fervent letter-writing campaign from fans persuaded the network to reverse itself—the first recorded instance of an audience campaign saving a doomed TV show. But it was only a temporary reprieve. For its third season, the show's budget was cut, Roddenberry stepped away from day-to-day involvement, and by most lights the show's quality declined drastically. By the end of season three, cancellation was a foregone conclusion.

In its three seasons, *Star Trek* had produced just 79 episodes, but that was enough to sell the reruns in syndication. There they proved amazingly popular, and pressure started to build to bring the series back. Instead, prompted by the success of *Star Wars*, Paramount (which had acquired the rights to the series from Desilu, the studio that originally produced it) decided to give the *Star Trek* crew a shot at the big screen. The 1979 feature *Star Trek: The Motion Picture* was only a middling success, but its 1982 follow-up, *Star Trek II: The Wrath of Khan* (with Ricardo Montalbán re-creating a villain he had played in a *Trek* episode from season one), was a hit both with critics and at the box office. The franchise began expanding at warp speed.

The new iterations surpassed the rather crude original series in many ways. *Star Trek: The Next Generation*, with an entirely new crew and cast headed by Royal Shakespeare Company actor Patrick Stewart (and with Roddenberry back in charge), boasted higher production values and more sophisticated sci-fi plots, not to mention better ratings than the original ever got. And the fourth series, *Star Trek: Voyager*, which debuted in 1995, rectified one major shortcoming of the earlier versions: for the first time, a woman (Kate Mulgrew) was in command of the ship.

Still, the original series boldly went where few TV shows of its day were going. Its multicultural, multiracial cast was itself a statement on diversity. "Intolerance in the 23rd century? Improbable!" said Roddenberry. "If man survives that long, he will have

learned to take a delight in the essential differences between men and between cultures." When *Pravda* complained that the international space crew included no representative of the Soviet Union, Roddenberry added Walter Koenig to the cast in season two, as the Russian navigator Chekov.

The space adventures, moreover, were often thinly disguised allegories for very current social problems. In one episode, "Let That Be Your Last Battlefield," the *Enterprise* crew encounter a planet, all of whose inhabitants are black on one side, white on the other. Yet they are riven by racial hatred between those who are black on the right half and those black on the left—a stark, if hardly subtle, condemnation of racial prejudice. In the Cold War–themed "A Private Little War,"

"Television was so tightly censored that science fiction was the only way to escape the taboos in politics, religion or anything else that was controversial," Roddenberry said. "I really don't consider myself a science-fiction writer, but I'm interested in what's happening on this planet and what may happen. In our society, we're treating man less and less like an individual and more like a social organism."

Roddenberry's utopian vision was not always reflected behind the scenes. Several writers for the show, among them the prominent sci-fi author Harlan Ellison (who wrote the classic time-travel episode "City on the Edge of Forever"), fumed at Roddenberry's habit of rewriting scripts so they would conform to his strict conception of the show's characters and message. Some cast members complained in later years about Shatner's camera-hogging ego and his jealousy of any co-star (especially Nimoy) who upstaged him with more lines.

Nor did the actors always welcome being typecast for an entire career, forced to reprise their characters for years in front of *Trek* nerds whose obsessive devotion to the show had its creepy side. Shatner himself expressed it memorably in a *Saturday Night Live* sketch from 1986. Appearing at a *Star Trek* convention, TV's Capt. Kirk gets testy after too many trivia-obsessed questions from fans. "Get a life!" he finally blurts out to the shocked fans—before being chastised by a convention organizer and returning to the microphone to claim that he was, of course, just playing the "evil Capt. Kirk" from the episode "The Enemy Within."

The fans were relieved. Shatner, in the sketch and real life, seemed resigned to his Kirkian destiny. And *Star Trek*—the show, the movies, the franchise, the cult—achieved a feat that even a Vulcan mind meld couldn't have foreseen. It lived long and prospered.

Richard Zoglin is TIME's *theater critic and the author of* Hope: Entertainer of the Century.

Kirk faces a dilemma over whether to supply arms to a primitive people engaged in a guerrilla war, to match the guns the Romulans have given to their enemies. In another episode, Kirk is taken captive by the Romulans and held as a spy after the *Enterprise* strays into the neutral zone—a story inspired by the then-recent North Korean capture of the U.S.S. *Pueblo*.

50 Years: A Long and

SALT MONSTERS, SPACE SHUTTLES, SHAKESPEAREAN ACTORS

January 1972
The first *Star Trek* convention is held in New York City. Sci-fi guru Isaac Asimov attends.

September 1966

NBC broadcasts the first episode, "The Man Trap": Kirk outwits a salt-loving alien who has eyes for McCoy.

1969 After 79 episodes, NBC cancels the series.

1975 Leonard Nimoy writes *I Am Not Spock*.

November 1979 *Star Trek: The Motion Picture* is released. The franchise lives!

November 1986 *Star Trek IV: The Voyage Home* premieres. In 1980s San Francisco, Spock and Kirk save the whales.

June 1989 *Star Trek V: The Final Frontier*, directed by William Shatner himself, is released.

1960   1970   1980

1964 Desilu Studios tries to sell *Star Trek* to CBS, which declines and decides to air *Lost in Space* instead.

March 1967 McCoy says, "I'm a doctor, not a brick-layer"— first variation of this phrase.

December 1967
"The Trouble with Tribbles": peak of *Star Trek* humor.

1967 Even at its ratings peak, *Star Trek* ranks No. 52, behind such shows as *Mr. Terrific* and *Iron Horse*.

Summer 1968 NBC announces the cancellation of the series but receives 1 million letters of protest and renews it.

November 1968 TV's first interracial kiss takes place between Kirk and Uhura. Censors insist on "no racial overtones," no open mouths.

1976 After receiving thousands of letters from Trek-kers, NASA names its space-shuttle prototype *Enterprise*.

June 1984 *Star Trek III: The Search for Spock*. Spock lives!

1987 TV series *Star Trek: The Next Generation* debuts, with Shakespearean actor Patrick Stewart on the bridge and an android riding shotgun.

December 1982 *Star Trek II: Wrath of Khan* is released; it features Kirstie Alley and Ricardo Montalbán's cleavage. Spock dies.

Prosperous Journey

AND SPINOFFS ALL BECAME PART OF THIS GALACTIC ADVENTURE

October 1990 With its 80th episode, *TNG* surpasses the original series's run. Classic *Trek* fans are aghast.

January 1993 Spinoff series *Deep Space Nine* debuts. Alien soap opera.

November 1994 *Star Trek Generations*. Kirk dies. Really.

January 1995
Star Trek: Voyager premieres. Lost in space.

December 1998 The film *Star Trek: Insurrection* features Picard rebelling against the Federation—and receives mixed reviews from critics.

February 2015 Leonard Nimoy, who portrayed Spock for 47 years, dies at age 83.

December 2002 The box-office flop *Star Trek: Nemesis* is released in theaters. Picard and his crew make their final film appearance as they travel to Romulus, the Romulan home world.

May 2013 A sequel to J.J. Abrams's reimagined *Star Trek* is released, bringing aboard Benedict Cumberbatch as Khan.

August 2016 The Rio Suites Hotel in Las Vegas is to host the five-day Official *Star Trek* 50th Anniversary Convention.

July 22, 2016 Premiere date of *Star Trek Beyond*. Directed by Justin Lin, it's the third installment of the reboot film series. Idris Elba joins the cast.

2000   2010   2020

March 1992 "Star Trek the Exhibition" opens at the National Air and Space Museum and becomes its most heavily attended exhibit ever.

November 1996 *Star Trek: First Contact* premieres, directed by Jonathan Frakes. The Borg make their big-screen debut opposite Capt. Picard and crew.

May 2005 After 98 episodes, *Star Trek: Enterprise* is canceled because of poor ratings.

October 1991
Gene Roddenberry dies.

September 2001 *Star Trek: Enterprise* premieres; the television prequel series takes place 100 years before the original series.

May 2009 Director J.J. Abrams premieres *Star Trek*. The film, which grosses more than any other *Star Trek* movie, stars Chris Pine and Zachary Quinto as Kirk and Spock from the original series.

January 2017
CBS is to release a new *Star Trek* television series that will be aired on its streaming service.

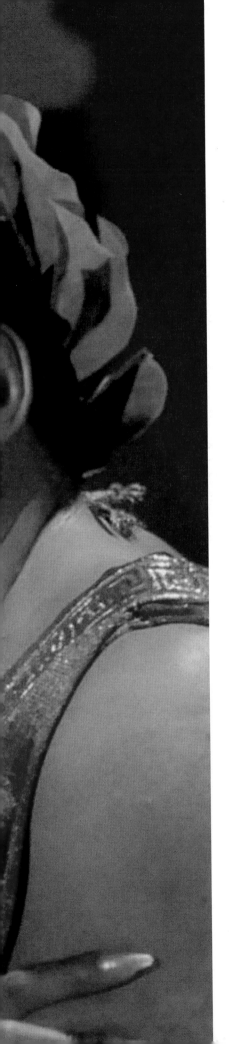

DIVERSITY ON THE BRIDGE

STAR TREK'S VISION OF HARMONY HELPED FANS EMBRACE THEIR OWN DIFFERENCES—AND WOULD BECOME A TOUCHSTONE OF THE SHOW FOR DECADES

BY ELIANA DOCKTERMAN

MARTIN LUTHER KING JR. WAS A TREKKER. IN FACT, IT WAS KING who persuaded *Star Trek*'s first African-American actress, Nichelle Nichols, who played Lt. Uhura, to stay on the show past the first season. The two met at a fund-raiser—to Nichols's shock, he made his way across the floor to her. King told her that *Trek* was the only show he and his wife, Coretta, would allow the kids to stay up and watch, that he was her biggest fan. When she informed him that she planned to leave the show and pursue a career on Broadway, he argued for the importance of a black character on the bridge.

"He just stared me in the eye and said, 'Do you understand what God has given you? What your role means for people of color watching back home? You have the first important non-stereotypical role,'" Nichols recalled recently. "'If you leave, they can replace you with a blonde-haired girl, and it will be like you were never there. What you've accomplished for all of us will only be real if you stay.'"

For King, and for millions of viewers since, *Star Trek* gave life to that future where skin tone, gender and nationality did not matter. Nichols decided to stay with the show, and in 1968, in the third

The episode "Plato's Stepchildren" (1968) is notable for sparking controversy over an interracial kiss between Uhura and Kirk.

From left: cast members Walter Koenig (Chekov), James Doohan (Scotty), Nichelle Nichols (Uhura) and George Takei (Sulu) appear at a *Star Trek* convention in 1976.

season, she and William Shatner shared what cultural historians believe was the first interracial kiss on a scripted television show.

In the 50 years since the original *Star Trek* series first aired, creator Gene Roddenberry's sci-fi story has made an indelible impact on American culture. Although *Star Wars* achieved a higher box-office gross and *Game of Thrones* boasts more viewers, *Star Trek* pioneered what a television show can mean to its audience, influencing fans, politicians and those who create our cultural content. The premise of the series—that people (and aliens) could overcome their differences for a common good—pushed the boundaries of network television in the 1960s. To varying degrees of success, each iteration of *Star Trek* since has examined social issues and politics and, in doing so, pushed other shows to take similar risks.

"*Star Trek* as a show never should have happened," says Anthony Rotolo, a professor at Syracuse University who teaches a *Star Trek* history course and has lectured at NASA's Johnson Space Center as well as the cultural convention South by Southwest. "In terms of racial diversity, gender diversity, it stuck out like a sore thumb on television at the time." The original starship *Enterprise* counted among its explorers an African-American woman (Nichols), a Japanese-American man (George Takei) and, beginning in the second season, a Russian (American actor Walter Koenig affecting a heavy Russian accent) at the height of the Cold War. (Bowing partly to commerce, Roddenberry cast Koenig both to make a political statement about U.S.-Russia relations and because of his resemblance to popular Monkees band member Davy Jones.)

What was truly radical, though, was that the show did not acknowledge how unique it was. "Roddenberry never discussed tokenism or quotas. He just made it the norm," Nichols says. "I never thought of myself as a black actress or a female actress, just a performer doing my best."

That's not to say that *Star Trek* was with-

In "Errand of Mercy" (1967), Kirk is embarrassed to admit that he made well-meaning but incorrect assumptions about the Organians, a non-corporeal race.

out inequality: the two main leads were white men, and the female characters sported short skirts and low necklines. "They were sexual objects," Kate Mulgrew, who played the first female captain on *Star Trek* in the 1990s, says of the early female characters. "Roddenberry was a genius, but he was a man. And he understood that sex sells, even in outer space."

Still, Nichols's Uhura was the chief communications officer of the *Enterprise*, not a homemaker. *Star Trek*'s contemporaries, family shows like *Leave It to Beaver* and *Bewitched*, not only took place in whitewashed, housewife-filled suburbia, they explicitly avoided controversy. "Those shows were designed as distraction. Roddenberry thought that was a lost opportunity. He wanted to challenge the audience," says Rotolo. "Then you look at the shows a few years down the road, shows like *Laugh-In* that are even more irreverent, and I think that speaks to *Star Trek*'s influence pushing the boundaries."

Roddenberry had a contentious relationship with *Star Trek*'s network, NBC. The previous show he'd created for them, *The Lieutenant*, had run just one season, in part be-

cause he insisted on filming an episode about racial discrimination in the U.S. military. It was only with the backing of Lucille Ball's production company, Desilu, that *Star Trek* got the green light to go to series on that network.

For three years, NBC nervously tested its willingness to go where no network had gone before. In an explicit plea for tolerance, the episode "Let That Be Your Last Battlefield" introduced an alien people divided into two groups, those with white on the right side of their faces and black on the left and those with the reverse coloration. Though the *Enterprise* crew members find this skin-color distinction to be inconsequential, the alien people battle each other over it, ultimately destroying their own planet.

As commendable as these plots may seem today, the 1960s American television audience didn't universally embrace *Star Trek*'s inclusive ideology. Affiliates in some Southern states refused to air that trailblazing kiss between Uhura and Kirk in "Plato's Stepchildren." As a result, it was the lowest-rated episode in the original *Star Trek* series.

In 1969, fans organized their first major meet-up, in a Newark, N.J., library. By 1972 they'd established a regular *Star Trek* convention where Roddenberry and sometimes the stars would greet fans, who wore homemade costumes like Spock's pointy ears— the birth of cosplaying, or dressing up like a favorite character. These gatherings only amplified Roddenberry's message of acceptance, one that echoed the philosophies of the civil rights movement and the second wave of feminism in that same time period. Fans gathered dressed as all different characters and types of creatures, regardless of race or gender. Decades later, 130,000 diverse and costumed fans roam the halls of Comic-Con International every year to celebrate their favorite genre films, shows and comic books.

Examine some of the most popular booths at Comic-Con, and you'll find traces of *Star Trek*'s legacy. George Lucas has said that *Star Wars* "stood on the shoulders" of *Star Trek*. Shows from *Babylon 5* (which was originally pitched as a *Star Trek* show, according to Rotolo) to Syfy's reboot of *Battlestar Galactica* have adopted the deep-space-diplomacy narrative. Less obviously, *Star Trek*'s structure influenced non-sci-fi procedurals. "TV shows that are dialogue-heavy and issue-heavy, like *The West Wing* and *Law & Order*, have become popular by following these complex, jargon-heavy conversations. *Star Trek* was the first show to do that," argues Rotolo. "Whether they're speaking in legalese or Shakespearean English or using scientific terms, you have characters solving complex issues in their field, and that's *Star Trek*."

Of course, the most obvious inheritors of the original *Star Trek*'s legacy are the other *Star Trek* shows that followed. Twenty years after the original *Star Trek*'s debut on NBC, the franchise was the most popular syndicated series on TV, thanks in part to William Shatner and Leonard Nimoy's *Star Trek* films. Paramount broadcast *Star Trek: The Next Generation* in first-run syndication from 1987 to 1994. The popular show embraced Roddenberry's mes-

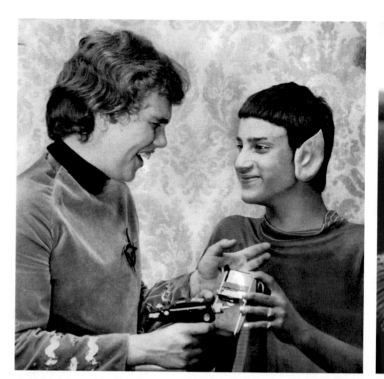

Clockwise from top left: Teenage fans impersonate Capt. Kirk and Mr. Spock at a 1976 convention in Canada; lieutenants Worf and Tasha Yar in the final episode of *The Next Generation* (1994); Kathryn Janeway, the captain in *Voyager* (1995–2001); the cast of *Deep Space Nine*'s second season (1993–1994).

sage of acceptance. Though once again, the two senior officers in *Next Generation* were white males, a female character, Lt. Tasha Yar, headed up the ship's security. The success of *Next Generation* led to the spinoff *Star Trek: Deep Space Nine*, which aired from 1993 to 1999 and featured an African-American man (Avery Brooks, playing Cdr. Benjamin Sisko) in command of the titular space station, aided by Nana Visitor playing Kira Nerys, a female second-in-command (and an alien, to boot).

But it wasn't until *Star Trek: Voyager* premiered in 1995 that a woman, Kate Mulgrew's Capt. Kathryn Janeway, was able to sit in the captain's chair. And while the network patted itself on the back publicly for its own progressiveness, behind the scenes, executives were nervous. "For many, many weeks, the networks came, and they stood on the soundstage and scrutinized me. They were waiting. I think they had a handful of [male] actors just waiting in the wings to jump into the captain's chair," Mulgrew says. "And each day they came, my resolve was strengthened."

Even as women were headlining their own shows, from sitcoms like *Roseanne* to sci-fi shows like *Xena: Warrior Princess*, they underwent a good deal of sexist scrutiny, particularly when it came to their looks. Just as *Voyager* hit the airwaves, Jennifer Aniston's much-copied hairstyle helped make *Friends* a breakout hit. Halfway through *Voyager*'s run, Keri Russell cut her hair on *Felicity*, launching dozens of news stories speculating as to whether the show's viewership would tank post-haircut. (It did.) *Star Trek* was no exception to such aesthetic analysis.

"I remember going to the executive producer and saying, 'Stop messing with my hair and my bosom and my outfit,' " Mulgrew says. "They changed my hairstyle seven times in that first season. 'You hired me because you thought I could do the job. Let me do the job.' Patrick Stewart didn't have that consideration. It was: you're a man, you're bald, let's go."

But despite numerous artificial changes, Kathryn Janeway remained one of the most robust roles for women in television at the time. As the leader of a stranded ship, the logical Janeway had to reconcile crew members and determine a path home. And at a

In *The Next Generation*, Lt.-Cdr. Geordi La Forge (left) is visually impaired. Lt.-Cdr. Data (right) is an android through whom the series explores the ethics of artificial intelligence.

time when women were still being blocked from prestigious science positions—a study commissioned by MIT the same year *Voyager* premiered found that just 8% of its School of Science faculty was female—*Voyager* emphasized that Janeway was a scientist at heart, drawn to explore the stars because of the discoveries she might make.

"I know she changed the lives of many women," says Mulgrew. "Hillary Clinton had me to the White House to speak about women in science. Female scientists watching *Voyager* were invited to think outside the box. They thought only men could be at the top of their field working with numbers, and all of a sudden the rules changed. I've spoken to women attending MIT who said, 'I don't want to just do research. I want to be the one to go into space.' It emboldened them."

Star Trek also served as inspiration for other groups. Geordi La Forge, the *Next Generation* character played by LeVar Burton (an actor who broke into the business on the seminal 1977 ABC miniseries *Roots*), was blind and used a high-tech visor to help him see. "I had a graduate assistant who was visually impaired and attributed much of the success of her life

to having that character as inspiration when she was young," says Rotolo.

Even our now-burgeoning discussion of android rights has its roots in *Star Trek*. The original series took an alternately positive and skeptical view toward technology. In "The Ultimate Computer," Kirk wonders what will happen if the ship's computer becomes so advanced that it's able to replace him, while Spock praises the computer's logic. (The computer winds up running amok and attacking other Starfleet ships.) *The Next Generation* presented the human-robot hybrid species the Borg as a main antagonist, human's fear of artificial intelligence rendered into a metaphor incarnate. The characters lasted throughout several versions of the series.

But the most sophisticated explorations of the computer-rights themes came in *Next Generation* stories centered on Data, an android member of the crew. A 1989 episode,

"The Measure of a Man," depicted a courtroom battle over the questions of whether Data should be accorded the rights of a sentient being. (Short answer: yes.) "One of the most beloved *Star Trek* characters of all time is a walking, talking computer with projected emotions," says Rotolo. "Today you have folks like [artist] Neil Harbisson in New York City, who is the first government-recognized cyborg—he was born unable to see color and has an antenna implanted into his head that allows him to hear color. *Star Trek* was really ahead of that and contemplated its moral implications." The conversation about whether artificially intelligent beings ought to be treated like humans has continued in modern films such as *Her* and *Ex Machina*.

For all of *Star Trek*'s success with diversity, some critics note that there is one topic that has remained relatively unexplored: no iteration of it has seriously addressed LGBT rights. "It's one of those glaring omissions," says Rotolo. "I know just from talking to folks in the show that they felt they never had a good script that was worth putting forward. Who knows the real reason." The closest *Star Trek* has ever come to issues of sexual orientation and gender identity was in a *Next Generation* episode titled "The Outcast," about a planet full of beings who have no gender. One of these beings comes out as a woman over the course of the episode, and a main character, Cdr. Riker, falls in love with her.

George Takei, the original series' Lt. Sulu and now a prominent gay-rights activist, says he once asked Roddenberry, who died in 1991, directly about the absence of gay characters on the show. According to the actor, the series creator feared backlash, especially after the famous interracial kiss. "That show was literally blacked out in the South—Louisiana, Alabama, Mississippi, Georgia didn't air that; our ratings plummeted," Takei said in an interview with the website Big Think in 2015. "And [Roddenberry] said, 'I'm treading a fine, tight wire here. I'm dealing with issues of the time. I'm dealing with the civil rights movement, the Vietnam War, the Cold War, and I need to be able to make that statement by staying on the air.' He said, 'If I dealt with that issue, I wouldn't be able to deal with

any issue, because I would be canceled.' "

Indeed, even now it is clear that LGBT issues remain *Trek*'s next frontier. And the feature-film reboots launched by director J.J. Abrams, while hugely successful at the box office, have led some fans to question whether future versions of *Star Trek* can stay true to Roddenberry's ideals. Some protested, for example, when the producers of *Star Trek into Darkness* cast the white actor Benedict Cum-

"STAR TREK IS ABOUT DIPLOMACY AND THE BATTLE OF THE HUMAN CONDITION."

berbatch in the role of Khan, a villain who was played by a person of color in the earlier *Wrath of Khan* film. More broadly, some fans complain that CGI-fueled shoot-outs have overshadowed *Trek*'s idealism. "Roddenberry famously said many times: If you want space battles, there are other films and other franchises out there for you. *Star Trek* is not that," says Rotolo. "*Star Trek* is about diplomacy and the battle of the human condition. It doesn't lend itself well to that kind of film."

That might change with a reboot of the show coming to CBS's streaming service, CBS All Access, in 2017. Though information on the new show is scant, Rotolo says that fans expect to see a non-heterosexual character in the main cast—and they'll let the network know if it fails to live up to their expectations. Gene Roddenberry's son, Rod Roddenberry, is producing the show, and he said in a press release that it will "uphold the tenets of *Star Trek*'s legacy." Given all of *Star Trek*'s accomplishments, that's no small feat.

Eliana Dockterman writes about culture and entertainment for TIME.

RACING TO SPACE

TREK'S FICTIONAL STARSHIP EMBARKED ON ITS JOURNEY WHEN NASA'S MISSIONS DOMINATED THE HEADLINES—FOREVER LINKING THEM BOTH

BY JEFFREY KLUGER

THE IMAGINARY EARTH OF *STAR TREK* WAS ALWAYS A NICER PLACE than the real Earth—especially the Earth as it was when the series was born. The starship *Enterprise* embarks from a united planet, which is itself part of a galactic federation that sends its explorers out into the universe. The Earth of the 1960s was a place on a knife edge, with the U.S. and the then–Soviet Union vying for global domination while hoarding enough nuclear weapons to reduce the planet to char. The space race itself was just one more expression of this very bitter conflict.

But give the old Cold Warriors this: when it came to space, they talked a good game. We would not militarize low-Earth orbit, we promised. We would not militarize the moon. In 1966 we negotiated an international agreement that went by the shorthand name the Outer Space Treaty but was formally known as the Treaty on Principles Governing the Activities of States in the Exploration and Use of Outer Space, Including the Moon and Other Celestial Bodies. Whatever it was called, it had a few simple rules, the most basic of which was: no cosmic combat.

While plenty of people were fooled by all the happy talk, however, not everyone was. The space race, while bracing, was a thing conducted by both sides in a state of mortal fear. The Soviets got

In 1976 *Star Trek* cast members join NASA officials for the unveiling of the space shuttle *Enterprise*, named for the iconic fictional spacecraft.

out to an early lead, launching Sputnik, the first satellite, atop their fearsome R-7 missile, a rocket that was far more powerful than anything in the U.S. arsenal and that would be just as happy to deliver a warhead to Toledo as a satellite to space. The U.S. responded to this muscle-flexing quickly, launching its

SPACE MADE US FEEL POWERFUL AND FEARFUL AND IMPOSSIBLY HUMBLE ALL AT ONCE.

first astronauts aboard the Redstone, Atlas and Titan boosters—weapons of war all. The astronauts who flew atop the Titans could actually feel the guidance system wagging the nose of the missile left and right, vainly sniffing for targets on the ground even as it was being aimed toward space.

Yet there was no denying that space would always be something more than just another arena of combat. There was the beauty of it, yes, the dreaminess of it. But there was also the enormity of it. Human beings, perverse animals, measure their power by their ability to break things. A single bomb can destroy a city. But set one of them off in space? A popgun. Space made us feel powerful and fearful and impossibly humble all at once, and we didn't know quite how to reckon with such a mix.

And into that swirl stepped *Star Trek*. It would be too much to say that the show was a cultural phenomenon from the start; it wasn't. It was the most-watched program in its 8:30 time slot on the evening the first episode aired—Sept. 8, 1966. That was a victory for the home network, NBC, but the win came cheap: in the same hour, CBS was airing the shopworn sitcom *My Three Sons*. *Star Trek*'s reviews were mixed—and some were dismal.

The *Boston Globe* called the show "clumsily conceived and poorly developed." The *Houston Chronicle* described it as "disappointingly bizarre." The *New York Post* fretted that the whole concept was just too intellectual. "One may need something of a pointed head to get involved," wrote the paper's critic.

But *Star Trek* had other things going for it that the critics overlooked. It had timing, for starters. On the very morning those reviews were coming out, NASA was preparing for the launch of Gemini 11, the 15th American spaceflight and one with grand plans—not the least being the distance the astronauts would travel from Earth. According to the *New York Times*'s front-page story, the spacecraft would "swing out farther into space than man has ever ventured—865 miles."

If you loved the space program and you watched that first episode of *Star Trek*—and plenty of Americans did both—the contrast was impossible to miss. The starship *Enterprise* could range across the galaxy, which is 621 quadrillion miles from one end to the other. The spaceship Gemini could go for 865 of those miles.

"When I was born, Sputnik had just been launched," says Alan Stern, principal investigator for the New Horizons mission, which achieved the first-ever flyby of Pluto, in July 2015. "At the time, 200 miles in altitude was the state of the art. *Star Trek* could have made that feel unimportant, but somehow it didn't. Even early on, it was more of a challenge to our better selves."

The show's curious ability to pose that challenge wasn't thanks to its sets or its costumes or its special effects, which were hopeless by modern-day standards and cheesy even by 1966 standards. Compare the visual style of the series with the dazzle of *2001: A Space Odyssey*, which hit movie theaters just two years later. Not even close. But while *2001* was eye-popping, it was also ponderous—space travel as undergraduate philosophy seminar. *Star Trek* was space travel as uplift.

"It was all in the scripts," says Stern. "It was all in the stories. The future that *Star Trek* depicted seemed like a technologically plausible one, and the characters were dealing with real issues, ones we could understand."

One of those issues—acutely apt in the era in which the show was born—was human tribalism. In the 1960s, television was integrating, though slowly, grudgingly. The drama *I Spy*, which premiered in 1965, paired Robert Culp and Bill Cosby as wisecracking intelligence agents—a black-white partnership that was revolutionary at the time. *The Man from U.N.C.L.E.*, which began the year before, was in some ways more daring, teaming an American secret agent with a Soviet sidekick. Beyond that, though, there wasn't much.

Star Trek famously exploded that cautious incrementalism. Yes, the captain was a white American male. But the ship was peopled by a multi-culti festival of skin shades and nations, crew members from Russia and Africa and Asia and Scotland and, just in case the entire color wheel of humanity wasn't enough, a Vulcan. The pioneering inclusiveness of *Star*

Trek was the polar opposite of the with-us-or-against-us, U.S.-Soviet nationalism that defined the real space race.

"I wasn't even born when the first *Star Trek* aired, but I know it resonated," says Italian astronaut Samantha Cristoforetti, who flew a 200-day mission aboard the International Space Station from November 2014 to June 2015, breaking the single-mission longevity record for a female astronaut. "It was at the end of European colonialism, and here you have an international crew that talks about its Prime Directive—the idea that you should go and explore but you shouldn't interfere with a culture to the point that you derail its development. Those things were a statement on what was going on in the world."

It was a statement that spoke loudly to Cristoforetti. She did not tumble for *Star Trek* until the 1990s, when she was in high school—but she fell hard. "I came to the U.S. when I was a student, at 17," she says, "and I thought I was in paradise because *Star Trek* was on twice a night. My host mother in Minnesota knew she had to give up the TV for those two hours."

Cristoforetti never shook off the spell. When she found herself in space in 2015, on the 20th anniversary of the premiere of the *Star Trek: Voyager* spinoff, she posed in the station's multi-windowed cupola in the Starfleet uniform of the show's Capt. Janeway, the first woman in the lead role of starship commander in the history of the series. A *Star Trek* costume is not something you have on hand in orbit unless you've planned it for a while.

Star Trek did not just have its effect person by person, child by child, as it did for Stern and Cristoforetti. Years after the first series ended and well before all of the movies and spinoffs were created, it had already seeped into America's national consciousness. By 1972, the Apollo program had ended, strangled for lack of funds. But the fact that we'd been to the moon could not be changed, and the fever dream of an even grander future, partly sustained by a vision like *Star Trek's*, could not be cooled so easily.

In 1976, NASA rolled out the first of what would eventually be six new space shuttles. That initial model was not intended to fly in space; rather, it was a trial vehicle that would be used to wring out problems and design flaws before the first vehicle actually did go into orbit. Nevertheless, it was a beautiful piece of engineering, and like any good vessel it needed an equally beautiful name. On September 3 of that year, White House senior economic adviser William Gorod sent

President Ronald Reagan, in a tan suit, waving from a platform by the prototype space shuttle *Enterprise*, joins nearly half a million spectators at Edwards Air Force Base in California to celebrate the landing of the space shuttle *Columbia* on July 4, 1982.

a memo to President Gerald Ford, making it clear what his choice should be.

"NASA has received hundreds of thousands of letters from the space-oriented 'Star Trek' group asking that the name 'Enterprise' be given to the craft," he wrote. "This group comprises millions of individuals who are deeply interested in our space program. Use of the name would provide a substantial human interest appeal."

Other staffers weighed in, agreeing with the idea. And although they also cited the deep roots the principle of enterprise has in the American economic system and the multiple times the name has been used for Navy vessels, the real reason was inescapable. The president took his advisers' advice, and on September 17 the new ship was rolled out of its Palmdale, Calif., hangar and formally named. Much of the cast of the original series, including DeForest Kelley, George Takei, Nichelle Nichols and Leonard Nimoy, were in attendance.

It was Nimoy more than any of the others—more even than William Shatner, who played Capt. Kirk—who was important to have on hand for the event, because it was Nimoy's Mr. Spock character that most deeply touched the culture. The complexity of the Spock character was all about contradiction—the push-pull between his logical and almost mystical sides. The 1960s were a time of widespread, if sometimes faddish, spirituality. But there was a binary—almost elitist—edge to the new enlightenment. To embrace spirituality you had to reject the empirical, the scientific, in search of something higher.

NASA's engineers and astronauts, however—empiricists all—were nothing like that. Many were more like Spock—and in some ways further along than Spock, with spiritual beliefs and scientific knowledge existing comfortably together. Buzz Aldrin performed a quiet communion in the Apollo 11 lunar module on the surface of the moon. The Apollo 8 astronauts read Genesis back to Earth while orbiting the moon on Christmas Eve in 1968. Charlie Duke, Apollo 16 moonwalker, returned to Earth and a few years later became a deeply devoted Christian. The most famous words spoken at the moment of John Glenn's first liftoff came from backup

The International Space Station, for now, is our starship *Enterprise*. Yes, it travels in circles instead of across the galaxy, and, yes, its maximum speed is 17,150 miles per hour instead of warp speed, which is faster than light. But nothing changes the ambition and scale of the thing—larger than a football field, which may not be *Enterprise*-size but is still more spaceliner than spacecraft. And nothing changes its collaborative ethos: the 15 nations that contributed hardware and labor to the construction job, the 222 different people from 18 countries who have spent time aboard.

In March 2016, NASA astronaut Scott Kelly and Russian cosmonaut Mikhail Kornienko returned to Earth after spending a year aboard

pilot Scott Carpenter, who intoned over an open mic, "Godspeed, John Glenn."

Certainly, a mere television character had little if any role in making those things happen, and Carpenter spoke his words four years before *Star Trek* ever aired. But it's not too much to say that a television character gave pleasing shape to the multiple dimensions—the profane and the divine—in all of us.

"I think Spock was the first embodiment of an alien persona that human beings ever took seriously," says Stern. "He was half-human, and that was part of the tension: logic versus devotion."

When Nimoy died in 2015, Cristoforetti, still aboard the International Space Station, tweeted down another picture of herself in the cupola, this time gazing out of the window while making Spock's signature "Live long and prosper" gesture. Quoting Capt. Kirk eulogizing Spock in the *Star Trek* movie *The Wrath of Khan*, she wrote: " 'Of all the souls I have encountered . . . his was the most human.' "

In 2014 NASA engineers unveils an artistic rendering of a future spacecraft for hypothetical warp speeds, an idea the agency has been investigating since 2010. The illustration was inspired in part by artist Matt Jefferies's original 1965 design of the starship *Enterprise*.

Space exploration today is an international cooperative. On Jan. 21, 2016, astronaut Scott Kelly of NASA (left) and cosmonaut Mikhail Kornienko of Roscosmos (right) mark their 300th consecutive day in space aboard the International Space Station.

the station. Training together for two years and flying together for one year, they were far beyond the old Cold War enmity of their parent nations, even in a time of increasing U.S.-Russian tension.

"I like to call him my brother from another mother," Kelly said about Kornienko before they left Earth together. That is both a peaceable and practical model for spaceflight, and it is one that will probably endure.

"I think that the eventual human presence on Mars will be multinational too," says Cristoforetti. "Just like with the station, there will always be different countries that can bring different things to the table."

When that interplanetary presence will occur, and whether it will reach beyond Mars and deeper into the galaxy, is unknowable for now. In some ways, we were spoiled by the Apollo era, when we simply willed a half-dozen lunar landings into being—and did it on a self-imposed deadline. But the accomplishment, grand as it was, may have been strangely premature.

"Arthur C. Clarke said that the 1960s were an anomalous decade," says Stern, "plucked out of the 21st century and plopped into the 20th." Once the U.S. won the space race, the old century could play out at its sleepier pace.

That may well be true, but *Star Trek*, which served as part of the soundtrack of that thrilling era, was no anomaly. Grand explorations have been part of our behavioral genome since our species first emerged. The tales we tell ourselves—in literature, in film, on television—help satisfy that impulse and help prod us to embark on those voyages for real.

Jeffrey Kluger, a TIME editor at large, co-authored Apollo 13 *with astronaut Jim Lovell.*

A STARSHIP FIELD GUIDE

AS THE *STAR TREK* UNIVERSE EXPANDED, SO DID THE NUMBER OF SHIPS CALLED *ENTERPRISE*. HERE'S A LOOK AT FIVE KEY ITERATIONS

NCC-1701
Constitution Class Starship

CONSTRUCTED AT: San Francisco Fleet Yards, Earth
LAUNCHED: 2245
FIRST SEEN IN: *Star Trek* (1966 TV series)
CAPTAIN: James T. Kirk

One of 12 ships in its original class, this Enterprise could cruise at warp 6 and exceed warp 8 in emergencies. Under Kirk's command, a succession of historic missions cemented its reputation as the Federation's flagship. Although its expansive hangar deck could accommodate multiple shuttle craft, its crew of 430 typically relied on transporter rooms to visit planet surfaces.

NCC-1701
Constitution Class Starship (upgraded)

REFITTED AT: San Francisco Fleet Yards, Earth
RELAUNCHED: circa 2270
FIRST SEEN IN: *Star Trek: The Motion Picture* (1979)
CAPTAIN: James T. Kirk

When the Enterprise returned to Earth after completing its five-year mission, it underwent an extensive series of renovations in an orbiting dry dock. Alterations—including new engine nacelles—changed the appearance of the ship substantially. Its journey ended in 2285 when Kirk used the auto-destruct sequence to keep it from being captured by Klingons.

NCC-1701-D
Galaxy Class Starship

CONSTRUCTED AT: Utopia Planitia Fleet Yards, Mars
LAUNCHED: 2363
FIRST SEEN IN: *Star Trek: The Next Generation* (1987)
CAPTAIN: Jean-Luc Picard

Advances in technology since Kirk's era resulted in a faster ship that, with more than 1,000 crew and passengers, was palatial compared with its 23rd-century namesake. Amenities included a bar named Ten-Forward, extensive holodeck facilities and a barber shop. In dangerous situations, its saucer section could separate and carry away non-Starfleet personnel while the drive section fought on, commanded from a special "battle bridge."

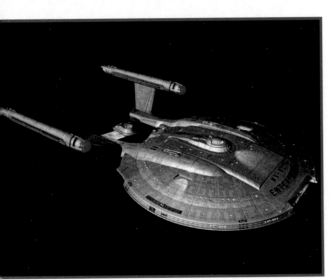

NX-01
NX Class Starship

CONSTRUCTED AT:
Warp 5 Complex, Bozeman, Mont., Earth
LAUNCHED: 2151
FIRST SEEN IN: *Star Trek: Enterprise* (2001)
CAPTAIN: Jonathan Archer

Designed to be Earth's first ship to exceed warp 5 speed and make interstellar exploration feasible, it carried a crew of 83. Its encounters with other cultures laid the groundwork for the formation of the United Federation of Planets.

NCC-1701 (alternative time line)
Constitution Class Starship

CONSTRUCTED AT: Riverside Shipyard, Iowa, Earth
LAUNCHED: circa 2258
FIRST SEEN IN: *Star Trek* (2009 film)
CAPTAIN: James T. Kirk

In an alternative time line caused by the arrival from the future of an older Spock and a Romulan, the Enterprise *retains the familiar twin-nacelle shape but displays a number of specific design differences, particularly in the interior. Initially commanded by Christopher Pike, it winds up being captained by Kirk, with Spock at his side.*

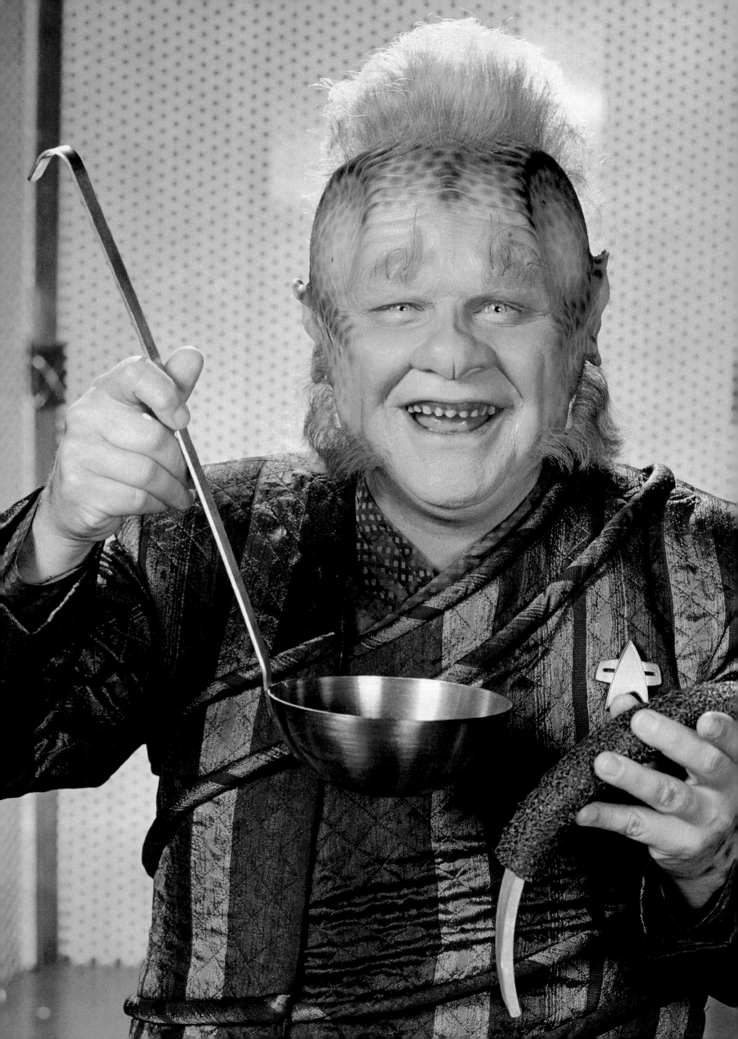

WAIT ... ARE THEY MAKING THAT UP?

FROM WARP DRIVE AND TRANSPORTERS TO MAGIC HEALING RAYS, *TREK*'S WRITERS LOOKED TO SCIENCE FOR INSPIRATION. WHAT'S REALISTIC, AND WHAT'S NOT?

BY JUSTIN WORLAND

I N THE SECOND SEASON OF *STAR TREK: VOYAGER*—THE FOURTH live-action television incarnation of the franchise—two key characters find themselves in a dramatic predicament. Tuvok (the ship's Vulcan security officer) and Neelix (a Talaxian who serves as local guide as well as ship's cook) are returning from an expedition to collect botanical samples from a nearby planet. When they are beamed back to *Voyager* along with some alien plant life, they wind up fused into a single being, who decides to call himself "Tuvix" to reflect his two constituent parts. *Voyager*'s doctor and officers spend the remainder of the episode figuring out how they might reverse the process—and whether it's ethical to do so.

In many ways, it's a typical *Star Trek* episode, with crew members in peril and a high-stakes moral dilemma. It's also exemplary in another way: the writers looked to actual science to find ideas for their science fiction. The creators intended the merging of the two characters to be a 24th-century extension of the theory of symbiogenesis, which 20th-century scientists developed to explain key aspects of evolution, explains André Bormanis, a writer and science consultant on the show. During symbiogenesis, two distinct organisms merge and form a symbiotic relationship. Current research

Actor Ethan Phillips stars as Neelix, the ship's cook, in *Voyager*. In one episode, Neelix is merged with Tuvok, a Vulcan, into a single being.

35

suggests that symbiogenesis was behind key aspects of the cells in our body, including the essential mitochondria, which provide energy to sustain life.

"That was front and center of the story," says Bormanis of symbiogenesis in the "Tuvix" episode. "Something like that

FOR WOULD-BE SPACE TRAVELERS, THERE'S A BIG PROBLEM WITH WARP DRIVE.

happened on a larger scale."

Throughout *Star Trek*'s 50 years of history, its writers have turned to science to find inspiration for their stories—and *Trek*, in turn, has inspired many fans to explore real-life science. "Half of the scientists and engineers that I've met or worked with have cited *Star Trek* as one of the big reasons they've gotten interested in science," says Bormanis. "You can use *Star Trek* as a teaching example of basic scientific concepts.

Of course, a futuristic space drama is at liberty to stretch the bounds of what's plausible, and *Star Trek*'s writers have made the most of that. At times, characters could veer into a barrage of technical dialogue that sounded science-y enough but seemed to provide more of a gloss of realism than any true insights about science. In fiction, that's known as "technobabble," and it was notorious enough in *Star Trek* that fans now refer to "Treknobabble." Still, in many cases, writers were drawing on hard science as the starting point for their tales, even when the onscreen portrayals turned out to be improbable or, in some cases, downright impossible.

WARP DRIVE, THE ENGINES THAT PROPEL *Star Trek*'s ships faster than the speed of light, may well be the show's signature science-fiction concept. For storytellers, warp

drive solves a critical problem: In a gigantic universe, how do you move your characters around swiftly to explore, as *Trek* promises, "new life and new civilizations"? Starships can activate warp drive when they need to make a quick escape or travel long distances—often between planets light-years away from each other. Ships traveling at "warp factor one" are traveling at the speed of light, or about 186,000 miles per second. (In contrast, NASA's New Horizons probe to Pluto—one of the fastest human-created craft ever—traveled from Earth to the edge of the solar system at about 10 miles per second.)

But for would-be space travelers, there's a big problem with warp drive. Albert Einstein's special theory of relativity, which explains the relationship between space and time, lies at the heart of the issue. The theory holds that the energy required to move—and accelerate—an object increases exponentially the faster an object is going. And, as an object goes faster, some of the energy applied to it turns into mass instead of inducing acceleration. The upshot: to move at the speed of light would require infinite energy. The theory has been tested—and confirmed—time and again, including in particle accelerators that fire tiny protons at up to 99% of the speed of light.

So is there any hope for the five-year missions of the future? Although scientists consider Einstein's special theory of relativity to be incontrovertible, some have looked for loopholes—theories that might reconcile relativity with light-speed travel. The most notable would require a spacecraft to contract space-time in front of it and expand space-time behind it. That method would employ negative matter, something that remains purely hypothetical—a far-out theory.

Even if warp drive is impossible, scientists are nevertheless inventing new and exciting ways to travel faster through space. Researchers funded by Russian billionaire

→

Crew members can be moved from ships to planet surfaces via transporters—fictional devices that beam beings as "energy patterns" (by way of low-budget special effects).

Yuri Milner are developing tiny space probes that will be able to travel close to the speed of light, using lasers to propel them. The method would reduce travel time to Mars to just a few days and could be ready to go in just a matter of decades, researchers say. And even though those devices will be far too small to carry humans, they would mark a significant step toward faster travel for other craft.

OK, maybe it's not so easy to get around the stars. But what about zipping around a planet—or, as was so often necessary in *Star Trek*, getting from an orbiting ship down to the surface? Capt. Kirk and his crew accomplished this with the transporter—a device that, along with the fading sound effect that it generates, ranks among the show's most iconic science-fiction technologies. The transporters, which are best thought of as teleportation devices, disassemble people in one location to create an "energy pattern" and then put them back together somewhere else.

Here, too, *Star Trek* writers were initially looking to solve a 20th-century conundrum: for a television show with a tight budget and only an hour to tell its stories, it was too costly in special effects and time to send crew members back and forth in shuttle craft. The transporter came to the rescue, instantly beaming characters everywhere with a relatively low-tech sparkle effect.

The problems with the concept of transporters are many and significant. "Dematerializing" a person—as it's known in *Star Trek* lingo—is theoretically possible under Einstein's mass-energy equivalence. Mass can be converted to energy, and vice versa, under the parameters of the equation $E = mc^2$. How you might actually go about that is anyone's guess—the amounts of energy would make an atomic bomb look like a firecracker. And good luck putting billions of particles back together at a new location exactly as they were before being dematerialized. "How would you store all the information? How would you even scan a person in a level of detail?" asks Bormanis incredulously. "I personally think it's crazy."

There's a more philosophical argument against the idea of a transporter: Would the person who emerges at the other end of the beam be the same person who was

From left: *The Next Generation* characters Deanna Troi, Geordi La Forge and William Riker prepare to enter the holodeck, a sort of virtual-reality system used for various purposes, such as training and entertainment.

dematerialized? Converting people into a stream of particles would, it seems, effectively kill them. That a molecularly exact duplicate would be constructed at the other end of the beam might offer little solace.

FOR A FUTURISTIC DEVELOPMENT THAT FEELS more grounded in today's high tech, consider *Star Trek*'s holodecks. These are essentially immersive virtual-reality rooms that crew members can use to experience practically anything they can imagine and travel to simulated versions of places both real and fictitious. On the surface, that sounds a lot like virtual-reality platforms such as Oculus Rift and HTC Vive that have popped up in recent years.

The virtual-reality systems of today represent a stunning advancement in immersive escape. Special goggles provide three-dimensional visuals, and clever audio technologies reinforce the illusion. But developing today's technology into holodecks represents a giant leap that is unlikely to occur anytime soon. The biggest problem may be that holodecks create a world that users not only see and hear but also touch and feel. The Treknobabble that was used to explain this alludes to "force fields" that created 3-D, touchable images that appeared to be solid. Today's virtual-reality pioneers think there may be ways to trick our sense of touch with air jets and pressure devices. But that still leaves the question of other sensations, such as the taste and smell of the food a holodeck participant consumes.

The holodeck environment also runs into stumbling blocks in the way it portrays artificial intelligence. The device allows users to interact with virtual humans and other creatures that technically do not exist but can think and respond intelligently. Artificial intelligence, which has advanced significantly since the dawn of *Star Trek*, remains far from sophisticated enough to offer a convincing depiction of a human being—though many computer experts believe machines may one day be able to think.

Meanwhile, current-day engineers continue to look for ways to get closer to the vision of a holodeck. At the University of Illinois at Chicago, researchers are experimenting with a virtual-reality space called CAVE2

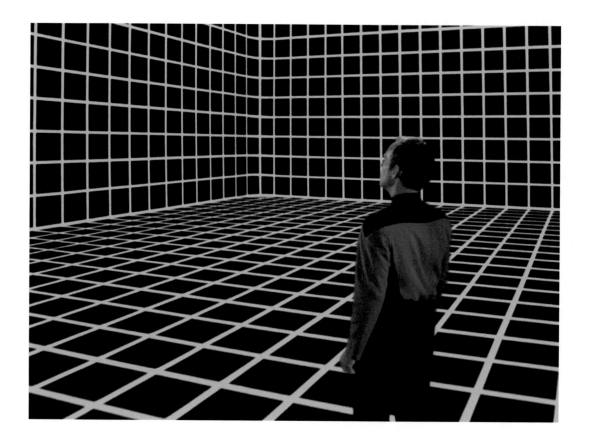

that places users in a room surrounded by liquid-crystal displays. Fittingly, one graduate student has already used it to reproduce a version of *Star Trek*'s *Enterprise.*

Lt. Reginald Barkley uses the holodeck in *The Next Generation* episode "Hollow Pursuits," which originally aired in 1990.

NO *STAR TREK* ACTION SEQUENCE WOULD BE complete without the ubiquitous phaser guns. Handheld versions of the devices shoot beams to kill enemies (they also have a "stun" setting to incapacitate bad guys without harming them); giant shipboard phasers target opposing vessels in *Trek* space battles.

Here on Earth, the science behind beam weapons is fairly clear and has been under development by the U.S. military and others for decades. Lasers rely on projecting a narrow stream of high-energy light onto a target, heating it up and destroying it. Many of the U.S. military tests are said to have been successes, but the devices have yet to enter into widespread use. And even the successful tests have worked only under controlled conditions and require large devices mounted on ships or aircraft.

The biggest problem for creating a hand-held phaser gun remains storing enough energy to actually power the device. With today's technology, a laser with the power to kill someone would require a huge battery, not one that can easily be lugged around. And that battery would heat up when fired, meaning a phaser user would probably require an additional device to keep the battery from overheating. Overcoming these hurdles may be feasible in the coming decades and centuries—the fundamental science is there—but for now, phaser development isn't practical.

If high-tech weapons can hurt people, are there high-tech ways to treat them? In *Star Trek*, healing rays can fix injuries—internal and external—with a simple flash of light that lasts a few seconds. The show doesn't explain the exact scientific justification for what seems like a medical miracle, but it turns out that small handheld devices that can treat some ailments already exist.

Phasers are energy weapons employed in the fictional universe; real laser weapon technology at *Trek* level is most likely a long way off.

Take a device under development by researchers at the University of Washington that uses ultrasound rays to seal holes in punctured organs. The device, about the size of a golf ball, plugs into a scanner held by a doctor. The doctor waves the device over the relevant body area, and invisible ultrasound waves heat the area until it becomes so hot that it fuses, closing the puncture. Researchers say it could be used to treat injuries to a variety of organs, from the liver to the kidney. The technology could transform a slew of surgical procedures—if and when it hits the market. A less dramatic version of ultrasound therapy that has been readily available for decades lets doctors use a handheld device to heat underlying tissue, which in turn can improve blood flow. Sports doctors and physical therapists in particular often rely on the treatment.

The devices and concepts in *Star Trek* illustrate how difficult it can be to hew to reality in extrapolating what science might achieve in the coming centuries. But that's also part of what has made the franchise so intriguing for generations of scientists. Bormanis, the writer and science consultant, says he loves when scientific inquiries "get people talking and raise questions."

And there are so many questions *Star Trek* has raised. The show's time frame is close enough that we can see the technological roots of what's to come but far enough away that it would be impossible to say much with any certainty. The concepts and plotlines in the show challenge the scientifically inclined to imagine what human ingenuity might uncover in the coming centuries. "*Star Trek* was supposed to be a very optimistic view of the future," says Bormanis. "I think it encouraged people to think about using science constructively to improve human life and improve the environment. And expand our opportunities."

Justin Worland writes about science and the environment for TIME.

THE FUTURE OF GADGETS IS NOW

FROM COMMUNICATORS TO TALKING COMPUTERS, *STAR TREK* TECH OFTEN ANTICIPATED—OR EVEN INSPIRED—REAL-WORLD ADVANCES

BY THOMAS E. WEBER

IMAGINE FOR A MOMENT THAT YOU HAVE THIS FAR-OUT FUTURISTIC gadget from the minds of science-fiction writers: a communications device small enough to be carried in a pocket or clipped to a belt. By activating it, you can speak to someone else practically anywhere on the planet, conducting a conversation with crystal clarity. The devices are ubiquitous, relied upon every day to keep people connected.

Of course, you don't have to work at all to imagine it. The device is called the cellular telephone, and it has been commonplace for 20 years now. But put yourself in the mind of a TV viewer sitting down to watch *Star Trek* in 1966. Earlier in the day, you thought about calling your friend from childhood who now lives a few hundred miles away, but you decided to wait until the weekend—it costs a lot to make a long-distance call, and rates are cheaper then. When you wanted to call home on the way from work to ask if there was still enough milk in the refrigerator, you had to pull the car over, find some change, get out of the vehicle and use a pay phone. But then you saw Capt. James T. Kirk whip out his Starfleet communicator

The tricorder, a handheld instrument carried by *Enterprise* crew members, has inspired a race to create a real-life sensor device that could gather information about the world.

and flip it open: "Kirk to *Enterprise*." No cords, no coins—just an instant connection.

Though much of the key science in *Star Trek*, like faster-than-light space travel and transporter beams, appears forever out of reach, when it comes to the show's gadgetry, the opposite has been true. Life in the 23rd and 24th centuries has consistently been outdone by things back here in the 21st. Computers that talk, digital libraries that can be accessed from anywhere, "replicators" that can create objects out of thin air—they've arrived far ahead of schedule. But of all the prescient *Trek* tech, it is the realm of communications that shows most clearly just how quickly the make-believe future can become real.

In 1973 Martin Cooper was an engineer working at Motorola, a big electronics company. He had a very terrestrial problem: telephone communication in the U.S. was controlled by "Ma Bell," the AT&T monopoly that would eventually be broken up following a government antitrust case. The idea of cellu-

Beings of the 23rd century use "communicators"—remarkably familiar handheld devices that allow wireless contact across great distances.

lar communication—a network of many radio transmitters and receivers that creates "cells," or sub-regions, rather than relying on one massive central antenna—had been kicking around for a while. One advantage of the approach was that any portable radio talking to the cell network didn't need to be unreasonably powerful. With one or more antenna sites in relatively close range at all times, it was feasible to create a reliable radio link with a small, portable device over a wide area. Ma Bell didn't seem that interested, though—it focused on radio telephones for automobiles, seemingly convinced that this service was mainly of use to a fairly small group of people whose jobs kept them in their cars for most of the day.

To Cooper, though, this cellular technology looked like nothing less than the future

of telephones. "For a hundred years we'd been trapped in our homes and our offices by the copper wire, and now we were going to be trapped in our cars," recalls Cooper, now 87. From his work on the burgeoning pager industry, he believed that millions would grab at a better way to stay in touch on the go. "The freedom that you get from personal communications—we had demonstrated that over and over again," he says. So he and his Motorola team produced a prototype handheld mobile phone that year. It would take years for it to evolve into a commercial product, but the future had been set in motion. The car phone would eventually become a relic, and the cellphone—still the size of a brick when wielded by Michael Douglas in the 1987 film *Wall Street*—would put a wireless communicator in everyone's pocket.

This, then, really was *Star Trek* brought to life. As phones got smaller, they got even Trekkier. Motorola's 1989 MicroTAC phone had a flip-open lid (though it flipped down,

the opposite of a Starfleet communicator). In 1996 came the phone certain to stir love in any Trekker's heart: a small, flat object that could be flipped open with the flick of a wrist, just like Capt. Kirk did. Motorola called it . . . the StarTAC.

The notion that Cooper was inspired by *Star Trek* has taken on mythical proportions, aided in part by his appearance in a 2005 documentary, *How William Shatner Changed the World*, which suggested that a *Trek* episode set off that little lightbulb of imagination above his head. Looking back now, Cooper says the legend has become a bit exaggerated—after all, he was steeped in the technology of communications through his work. And for fictional inspiration, he had an even earlier example: the wrist radio worn by comic-book detective

45

Bluetooth earpieces, tablet computers and virtual-reality headsets are a few of the real-life technologies foreshadowed by the futuristic series.

Dick Tracy starting back in 1946. Still, he says, those Starfleet-issue communicators looked pretty good to him. "I'm a science-fiction fan," Cooper says, "and I would not suggest that *Star Trek* wasn't an influence."

Cellular telephones, it turns out, were just the beginning. The bigger the market for personal communications has grown, the more *Star Trek*'s onscreen gadgets have come to seem positively prophetic. Consider the wireless earpieces used aboard the *Enterprise*. Stuck into an ear, these cylindrical silver devices let Lt. Uhura hear incoming transmissions while keeping her hands free to operate the controls at her station. In 1994 a Swedish telecommunications company introduced a short-range wireless technology designed to link nearby components. It was called Bluetooth—and now it's everywhere. It has become the enabling protocol for a wide range of computer and phone accessories, including tiny wireless earpieces that make Uhura's 23rd-century version look antiquated. They sell for $20 or less.

On the ship, Kirk's crew often turned to video communications. The other party could be seen on the main viewscreen of the bridge or on smaller desktop displays. A three-sided unit in the *Enterprise* briefing room facilitated videoconferencing. Today, that capability is commonplace—whether it's an elaborate conference-room setup at a business or the Skype and FaceTime software that runs on computers and phones. Much like our 23rd-century counterparts, though, many people still find audio calls sufficient for most conversations.

Of course, as real-world technologies progressed, *Star Trek*'s creators had to keep advancing their conjectures of what the space explorers of the future would use. When *Star Trek: The Next Generation* premiered in 1987, the handheld communicators were nowhere to be seen on the new and improved starship *Enterprise*. Instead, characters were equipped with a piece of jewelry, typically worn on the chest, where it also served as the Starfleet uniform insignia. Called the combadge, it made communications utterly simple. Crew members tapped the badge and spoke aloud to initiate a conversation: "Picard to Riker." Though the visual design of the combadge would con-

tinue to evolve, it served as the main communications device through *Next Generation, Star Trek: Deep Space Nine* and *Star Trek: Voyager.*

Pretty cool—and perhaps, like Kirk's original communicator, closer to being a reality than it might seem. Google has already developed a prototype wearable communicator that can be worn as a badge on the chest and, you guessed it, turned on with a quick tap. Amit Singhal, the Google engineer behind the project, says the similarity of that prototype is no coincidence. "I always wanted that pin," Singhal told TIME in 2015. "You just ask it anything and it works." The communicator uses Bluetooth and can play audio to headphones or through a speaker. Singhal, who retired from Google in early 2016, is a devoted *Trek* fan; he gave another project at the company the code name Majel in honor of Majel Barrett Roddenberry, who died in 2008. (The actress was the wife of Gene Roddenberry and played Nurse Chapel along with voicing the *Enterprise* computer.)

There is one thing *Star Trek* failed to foresee about the phones of the future: that humans would become oddly addicted to them. You never saw Starfleet officers texting away while oblivious to their physical surround-

Amit Singhal models a Google prototype of a Bluetooth-enabled lapel-pin device modeled after the iconic *Star Trek* communicator badge.

ings. The closest thing to that ever depicted was a virtual-reality device in the *Next Generation* episode "The Game." Brought on board by Cdr. Riker, it swiftly gets nearly the entire crew hooked—and is then revealed to be part of an alien race's scheme to commandeer the *Enterprise.* Fortunately, the plan is thwarted by a quick-thinking Wesley Crusher.

COMMUNICATIONS WASN'T THE ONLY ZONE where *Star Trek* foreshadowed the devices to come. The show was equally farseeing in its depictions of information technology. In the late 1960s, computers were mainly the realm of businesses and universities; they filled entire rooms with their massive equipment racks. The onboard computer for the Apollo spacecraft then voyaging to the moon was considered a triumph of miniaturization—invented at the Massachusetts Institute of Technology, it weighed 70 pounds. Its entire memory could hold only the equivalent of a

Kirk and McCoy use a supposedly futuristic tablet computer. The clunky electronic clipboard is a far cry from an iPad, but the concept demonstrates the technological foresight of the *Trek* series.

few seconds of an iTunes music file.

Humans interacted with those '60s computers using punch cards and teletypes. Aboard the *Enterprise*, things were far simpler. Crew members spoke instructions to the ship's computer, which would respond with a synthesized voice or by showing information on a display. Today, chatty computers are beginning to appear all over the place. Amazon sells a smart-home gadget called the Echo that answers to the name Alexa and will start playing music or answer search queries in response to a voice command; Apple's Siri can converse with iPhone users to complete routine tasks.

What seemed even more futuristic was the apparent omniscience of 23rd-century information technology. The *Enterprise* com-

THE SHOW WAS FARSEEING IN ITS DEPICTIONS OF INFORMATION TECHNOLOGY.

puter, both in Kirk's era and later aboard Picard's ship, contained practically anything crew members might want to know—the ultimate library, available instantly all the time. Now we take for granted the massive repository of Wikipedia and the power of Google to find answers to all kinds of questions. And the USB flash drives we use to physically carry computer files are much more svelte than the "record tapes" from the *Enterprise*.

As for looking at readouts of all that information, folks on the 1960s *Enterprise* didn't have the most inspiring technology: junior officers would present Kirk reports to approve on one of the most unappealing tablet computers ever seen: a bulky black-box affair with a slanted top, seemingly meant to evoke an electronic clipboard rather than a tablet computer. (A more recognizable gadget in this category can be seen in the 1968 film *2001: A Space Odyssey*, in which the astronauts watch

video on a flat display called the Newspad.) By the *Next Generation* era, Starfleet had modernized its tablets into a touchscreen called the Personal Access Display Device, or PADD. The PADD came in a variety of sizes—just like Apple's iPad and Samsung's Galaxy tablets. But it's worth noting that an important forerunner of today's ubiquitous tablets, the Apple Newton MessagePad, arrived in 1993—while *Star Trek: The Next Generation* was still airing new episodes.

PLENTY OF OTHER EXAMPLES DEMONSTRATE the ability of *Star Trek*'s designs and gadgets to anticipate—or inspire—our real-world future. A unit of the U.S. military reportedly built a command center that strongly resembled the layout of the U.S.S. *Enterprise* bridge. (*Foreign Policy* magazine quoted a retired officer as saying, "Everybody wanted to sit in the chair at least once to pretend he was Jean-Luc Picard.")

Starfleet's medical technology looked so sensible that engineers are racing to mimic it for the 21st century. The Qualcomm Tricorder X Prize competition will award $10 million to a team that can create a tool, weighing no more than 5 pounds, to "accurately diagnose 13 health conditions." The competition has explicitly linked its work to *Star Trek*, showing images of Starfleet tricorders on its website and bringing actor Brent Spiner, who portrayed Lt.-Cdr. Data, onstage at an event. A winner is expected to be announced in 2017.

More seems certain to come. Silicon Valley hasn't yet built a "replicator" as magical as the Starfleet devices that can materialize a meal or a tool in seconds, but advances in 3-D printing suggest that the capability isn't far off. Language-translation software for smartphones is bringing *Trek*'s universal translator within reach. And artificial retina systems for the blind offer hope that Geordi La Forge's sight-restoring VISOR won't remain science fiction.

It was sci-fi author Arthur C. Clarke—who wrote *2001: A Space Odyssey*—who once posited this: "Any sufficiently advanced technology is indistinguishable from magic." Today, technology is advancing ever more rapidly—giving everyone some *Star Trek* magic centuries before its time.

This Enterprise

STAR TREK'S ENDURING POPULARITY HAS MADE IT A CULTURAL

TOURIST ATTRACTIONS

Star Trek canon says that James T. Kirk hails from Iowa—which led the city of Riverside to proclaim itself the captain's future birthplace. Visiting fans can snap their selfies at this marker.

IN YOUR MAILBOX

The United States Postal Service honored *Trek* with this *Enterprise* stamp in 1999. This year, it's commemorating the 50th anniversary with a set of four stamps.

OFFICE BUILDINGS

Any fan can dress up in a costume, but Chinese entrepreneur Liu Dejian loves *Trek* so much that he built a corporate center in Fujian province that mimics the shape of the *Enterprise*.

Goes Everywhere

BENCHMARK—DRAWING TRIBUTES BOTH SERIOUS AND WHIMSICAL

ON THE BIG SCREEN

Galaxy Quest, a 1999 film, is both a pitch-perfect parody and a loving homage to *Star Trek*. In it, Tim Allen plays a William Shatner–esque actor who once starred in a fictional TV show called *Galaxy Quest*, which real aliens have seen and believe to be "historical documents." The story includes send-ups of everything from redshirts to transporter beams.

IN SONG

For their 2004 song "Ch-Check It Out," the Beastie Boys riffed on the show in their lyrics ("All you Trekkies and TV addicts / Don't mean to diss, don't mean to bring static") and, wearing Starfleet uniforms, were beamed into the opening of the song's video.

ON THE SMALL SCREEN

Over the years *Saturday Night Live* has repeatedly spoofed *Star Trek*. This Shatner "get a life" segment may be the best known, but the 1976 sketch with John Belushi as Shatner refusing to step out of his Kirk character when NBC cancels the show is undeniably a classic.

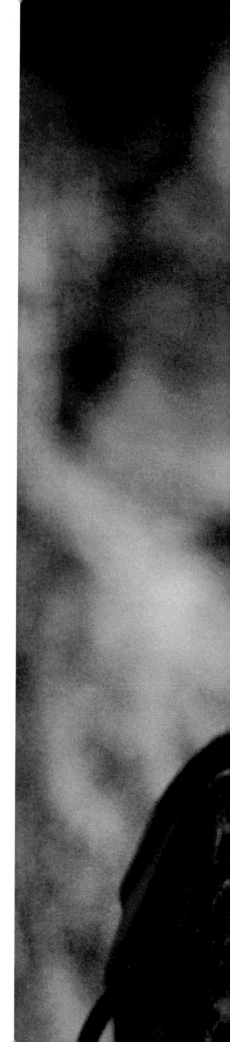

TO SEEK OUT NEW LIFE

KLINGONS. ROMULANS. ROCK CREATURES. OVER FIVE DECADES, *STAR TREK* HAS COME UP WITH SOME OF THE MOST ICONIC ALIENS EVER—AND SOME OF THE MOST COMPLEX, TOO

BY ALEX FITZPATRICK

SINCE THE TIME OF THE GREEK PHILOSOPHER ANAXIMANDER, humans have gazed up at the heavens and wondered: Is anyone else out there? For some, the idea that we might be the most advanced beings in all of creation offers a sense of supremacy. Others find it a lonely thought.

Reality has yet to offer a conclusive answer one way or the other, leaving our imaginations to run wild. If aliens do exist, what might they look like? How would they behave? And crucially: Would they be friend or foe? Thinkers no less great than the physicist Stephen Hawking have warned of the latter possibility. "If aliens ever visit us, I think the outcome would be much as when Christopher Columbus first landed in America, which didn't turn out very well for the Native Americans," Hawking remarked in a 2010 documentary on the subject.

Thankfully for the curious among us, science-fiction writers have stepped up to fill our imaginations with myriad possibilities.

In *Voyager*, actress Jeri Ryan plays a Borg— an alien race of cybernetic organisms that operate as a "Collective" that assimilates other species.

Their creations have extended far beyond the archetypical "little green men." H.G. Wells's 1898 *War of the Worlds*, widely hailed as an exemplar of the genre, gave us terrifying Martian invaders and their tripodal death machines. *The Day the Earth Stood Still* (1951) offered Klaatu, who visited Earth to urge humanity to end our warlike ways. And of course there was E.T., the disarmingly cute alien simply in need of a ride home.

But nothing in science fiction has contributed to the depth of the extraterrestrial encyclopedia like *Star Trek*. From the Bajorans (a proud people struggling to recover from another species's hostile occupation of their world) to the Tamarians (a seemingly incomprehensible race that turns out to communicate through mythology and metaphor), *Star Trek*'s writers have dreamed up nearly 300 different alien species and counting, according to the fan website Memory Alpha. And that's just the humanoids.

How can one franchise spawn so many aliens—and so many memorable ones, at that? Necessity, as they say, is the mother of invention. Science fiction typically uses spaceships, death rays and time travel as devices to offer ominous warnings about the ways humanity can go awry. *Star Trek* creator Gene Roddenberry flipped that script, introducing to a 1960s audience a future in which an integrated cast of humans (and, just to drive the point home, one actual alien) work together to better understand their universe.

That utopian vision was essential to *Trek*'s DNA, but it was also a tremendous challenge for one group of people: *Star Trek* writers, who faced the daunting task of writing stories in which the main characters all got along just fine.

"Gene was very big on not wanting to create conflict among the characters on the show," says Rick Berman, who led the *Star Trek* franchise after Roddenberry died in 1991 until 2005 and produced several series and feature films. "He felt that humans, especially Starfleet humans, had evolved to a point where he didn't want to see conflict between them."

Yet conflict is at the core of all great storytelling. So if the *Enterprise* crew couldn't

The M-113 creature, the last survivor of its race, is encountered and eventually killed in a 1966 episode.

Kor (right) is a Klingon, a militaristic humanoid species that serves as an antagonist in the original series.

Winn Adami is a religious leader from the planet Bajor in *Deep Space Nine*.

Dathon is a Tamarian, an alien race from the planet Sigma Tama IV, in *The Next Generation*.

squabble with one another, *Star Trek* writers had to find friction elsewhere. Aliens came to the rescue. "Often we were telling stories of how humans had progressed, or not, in the far reaches of space," says longtime *Star Trek* writer D.C. Fontana. "But sometimes the theme of the tale was better told by demonstrating how aliens approached or solved problems, or how they failed."

Things got off to a rocky start. Putting aside Spock—a full-fledged member of the *Enterprise* crew—the first extraterrestrial to appear on *Star Trek* was a C-list monster that could have been pulled from any bad '50s sci-fi flick. A shape-shifter with a serious salt craving, the nameless creature killed off *Enterprise* crew members by sucking the sodium out of them. The so-called "salt vampire" wasn't a big hit. Thankfully, matters improved from there.

HUMANS ARE COMPLEX CREATURES, CAPABLE of being logical, tactical, aggressive, greedy and lustful all in a single one-hour episode. But *Star Trek* aliens are typically guided by one prime mover. Often it is some trait shared by many people. A desire for conquest, perhaps, or the pursuit of wealth or the urge to protect one's offspring. That made them a thinly veiled stand-in for whatever driving force they represented, giving the writers a way to craft stories that were less about aliens and more about us. Simply put, *Star Trek* aliens are a mirror in which we see the best and worst of ourselves—and one in which we see that we're not as different from one another as we might think.

"The concept of having aliens on a week-to-week basis, sometimes new, sometimes ones that the audience was familiar with, gave the writers the ability to represent all the different qualities of humanity," says Berman. "Whether it's avarice or whether it's a hive-like mentality or whether it's emotions or whether it's a desire to be more human, these were all qualities that the aliens allowed us to play with. We could not have done the show without that."

Case in point: In the third-season *Next Generation* episode "The Survivors," Capt. Jean-Luc Picard and his crew find a couple who appear to be the only survivors of an attack on a Federation colony. But when they are offered safe harbor aboard the *Enterprise*, they refuse, insisting they be left where they were found. It's an odd request, given their situation. A series of other strange happenings, such as a warship appearing to drive the *Enterprise* away from the planet, convinces Picard that something is amiss with the pair, who are named Kevin and Rishon Uxbridge. Picard is eventually able to trick Kevin into revealing the truth: he's not a human but a member of an all-powerful species called the Douwd. Kevin admits that he created a fictional version of Rishon after she was killed

IN PART, STAR TREK *IS A* CELEBRATION OF HUMANITY'S INDIVIDUALITY.

in an attack by a murderous race called the Husnock. What's more, Kevin, who considers himself a pacifist, reveals that in his rage over losing his wife, he killed the Husnock. And not just the Husnock who attacked his world but all of them, everywhere in the universe.

Kevin's reaction is perfectly "human." Who hasn't wished ill will on those who do us wrong? The difference, of course, is that Kevin has the power to satisfy his rage to a horrific extent. Picard, typically motivated by justice, admits that the Federation has "no law to fit" Kevin's crime, instead letting him live in exile on the planet. The captain concludes, "We leave behind a being of extraordinary power and conscience. I am not certain if he should be praised or condemned. Only that he should be left alone."

With the possible exception of Spock and the rest of the Vulcans, *Star Trek*'s best-known aliens are the Klingons. A ruthless warrior race obsessed with battle and hon-

or, the Klingons originally served as a two-dimensional foil for Kirk and company. Many have viewed them as a bellicose stand-in for the great space-race enemy of the original series' era, the Soviet Union. But so popular have the Klingons become over the decades that theirs is the most widely spoken fictional language in the world, according to *Guinness World Records*. (Take that, *Lord of the Rings* fans.) There's even an ongoing copyright battle over who owns the Klingon language, which has generated some of the more entertaining legal briefs of our time.

At least some of the credit for that popularity is due to actor Michael Dorn, who played the Klingon bridge officer Worf in *The Next Generation*. That series took the original, more-cartoonish Klingons and gave them depth and relatability. Klingons, as it turns out, are a lot like us. The Klingons are warmongers, like some humans. The Klingons are obsessed with rituals, like some humans. The Klingons are driven by a fierce dedication to their family, like some humans. One of *Star Trek*'s best Klingon stories came in "Sins of the Father," a third-season *Next Generation* episode in which Worf's late father is accused of treason. As much as it pains him to do so, Worf decides to shoulder the blame in accordance with Klingon custom, despite his father's innocence, a move that will help preserve the Klingon Empire's political status quo and keep the empire from spiraling into chaos that could ultimately harm millions. It's a deeply human story, a meditation on family pride as much as it is a revealing look into the intricacies of Klingon politics.

IF THE KLINGONS WERE *STAR TREK*'S ORIGINAL villains, the Borg were the show's best. A technologically advanced race of cyborgs, the Borg are bound together into a hive mind called "the Collective." Just looking at the Borg, a terrifying hodgepodge of man and machine, is enough to send shivers down your spine. But the real terror lies in their motivation: intergalactic racial purity. When the Borg encounter a new species, they either add it to the Collective through forced "assimilation" or simply kill it off.

Col. Worf (played by actor Michael Dorn) is a Klingon defense attorney in 1991's *Star Trek VI: The Undiscovered Country*.

It's unclear which is the worse fate. In part, *Star Trek* is a celebration of humanity's individuality. The Borg are everything *Trek*'s humans are not: obedient, robotic, conformist. So great is the fear of assimilation that in the *Star Trek* film *First Contact*, an *Enterprise* crew member who's going through the horrific process begs Capt. Picard to kill him out of mercy. Picard—who had once been assimilated himself but was saved in a daring rescue by his crew—obliges. "The concept of being assimilated was terrifying, because it seemed like you had no control over it and no ability to combat it," says Jonathan Frakes, who played *Star Trek*'s Cdr. William T. Riker and directed *First Contact* as well as *Star Trek: Insurrection*.

The Borg, who first appeared in a 1989 episode of *The Next Generation*, are typically considered a commentary on fascism and racial cleansing. But in a sense, they are aliens posing questions we didn't even realize we would soon be facing. Can we real-world humans be addicted to constant connectivity through our smartphones, as the Borg are to the Collective? (Cut a Borg off from the hive mind, and the alien's nonplussed reaction is not unlike that of a teenager stripped of an iPhone.) Does social media give us a platform on which to connect with others to enhance our common understanding, or does it create a hive mind that rejects unpopular opinions, as does the Collective? Should we enhance our physical and mental capabili-

Quark (played by actor Armin Shimerman) is a bar owner and a Ferengi—a humanoid alien species from the planet Ferenginar—in *Deep Space Nine*.

ties with technological implants, as the Borg do? Watch the Borg stories with these pressing questions in mind, and they only become more fascinating.

GIVEN THE PROMINENCE OF RACES LIKE THE Klingons and the Borg, it might seem as if *Star Trek*'s aliens are almost always villains. That's far from the case. The greedy Ferengi, introduced early in *The Next Generation*, were intended as such at first. But fans considered them too silly to be a serious threat. Instead, the Ferengi soon turned into walking, breathing commentaries on the advantages and flaws of unbridled capitalism. If Donald Trump were a *Star Trek* alien, he would be a Ferengi. They're driven entirely by making money; they always want the better part of the deal. (They also happen to be some of the most sexist creatures in *Trek*: they outright ban women from business, though their society undergoes reforms as their story line progresses.) These characteristics put them in stark contrast with *Star Trek*'s humans, who work not for money but "to better ourselves and the rest of humanity," as Capt. Picard once put it.

Star Trek's quintessential Ferengi was Quark, a seedy intergalactic businessman and bartender who was brought to life by actor Armin Shimerman in *Deep Space Nine*, the franchise's third television series. Quark often quoted from "the Rules of Acquisition," a sort of Ferengi guidebook that could double as Gordon Gekko's personal manifesto. Example rules include "Never place friendship above profit," "Never allow family to stand in the way of opportunity" and "War is good for business." But *Deep Space Nine*'s writers went beyond using Quark as a mere punching bag for Wall Street. In the season-three episode "The House of Quark," for instance, we see him use his business-like cunning to escape certain death in a duel with a Klingon. The lesson? Sometimes greed is good.

Star Trek writers were skilled at constantly adding depth to the aliens who reappeared through the series. Just as the Klingons' belligerence was leavened with stories about their love of honor, the warlike Romulans turned out to be literally related to the Vulcans—a glimpse at *Trek*'s most logical race with the superego dialed back and the id given more say. But even the lesser aliens could force viewers to look beyond the surface. In the original series's "The Devil in the Dark," a murderous rock-like creature called a Horta turned out to be killing only to protect her young. *The Next Generation*'s "11001001" brought us the Bynars, a computer-dependent race who

IF DONALD TRUMP WERE A STAR TREK ALIEN, HE WOULD BE A FERENGI.

worked only in pairs, providing a lesson about the power of cooperation. And *Star Trek: Voyager*'s "Year of Hell" offered the history-alerting Annorax, who aimed to use his time weapon to restore his people's empire to its former glory but killed his own wife in the process, revealing the cost of stubborn pride.

On one level, *Star Trek* is a science-fiction show about a group of intellectually enlightened humans exploring the far reaches of the galaxy, all to better their understanding of their world. But the show is really about us, back here in the present day, and the common ties that bind us. What better way to show us we're all alike than through the lens of outsiders? "Aliens are really important in science fiction because they give a little distance character-wise and story-wise so that you can actually have stories about beauty and youth and racism, and on and on and on," says John de Lancie, who played *Star Trek*'s godlike character Q. "It puts it on the character of an alien to be able to say things that sometimes you can't say straight out. I think the aliens in *Star Trek* and the aliens in most science fiction have a lot of value in that respect."

Alex Fitzpatrick is deputy technology editor at TIME.

Top 10 Aliens of the

VULCANS, ROMULANS AND TRIBBLES, OH MY! HERE ARE THE SPECIES

VULCAN

Planet: Vulcan
Powers: Nerve pinch, mind meld
Notables: Spock, Sarek, T'Pau

Though known for devotion to logic and reason over emotion, the Vulcans have a history of extreme violence and aggression. Surak, a revered figure, preached a philosophy of logic, which came to dominate Vulcan and fuel its sophisticated civilization. An offshoot group who rejected Surak's teachings founded Romulan society.

Appeared in: *TOS, TNG, DS9, VOY, ENT*

FERENGI

Planet: Ferenginar
Favorite object: Bars of latinum converted to gold, a currency
Notables: Quark, the Grand Nagus

A culture of ultra-capitalists, the Ferengi are primarily focused on commerce. The Rules of Acquisition provide a code for all Ferengi to become successful and profitable; cosmetically enlarged earlobes are signs of wealth. Their greed has allowed them to stay neutral in galactic conflicts. Their male-dominated society is taking early steps toward equality.

Appeared in: *TNG, DS9, VOY, ENT*

KLINGON

Planet: Q'onoS
Weapon of choice: Bat'leth, the Sword of Honor
Notables: Kor, Worf

Combative and driven by honor, the Klingons are one of the leading military forces in the galaxy. The Klingon Empire is seemingly resource-poor, which contributes to a conquest-oriented mentality—and decades of hostility with the Federation and the Romulan Empire, in spite of erratic alliances. The Klingons eventually allied with the Federation to defeat the Dominion.

Appeared in: *TOS, TNG, DS9, VOY, ENT*

CHANGELING

Origin: Gamma Quadrant
Powers: Shape-shifting, the Great Link
Notables: Odo

Morphogenic enzymes give these beings the ability to shape-shift. Changelings can take on any form, even a cloud of fog. The Founders, a group of Changelings, forged the Dominion in an attempt to stabilize the chaos around them. Despite their power, the Founders don't care much for individual identity and consider themselves parts of a larger unit.

Appeared in: *DS9*

CARDASSIAN

Planet: Cardassia Prime
Notables: Gul Dukat, Elim Garak, Damar

Treacherous and aggressive, the Cardassians have battled the Federation, Romulans and even the Klingons. Despite a penchant for combat, Cardassians highly regard the arts. But the price of the culture's militancy has been high: the race fought three major wars in a century, the third resulting in the loss of almost a billion Cardassian lives.

Appeared in: *TNG, DS9, VOY, ENT*

KEY: *TOS*: THE ORIGINAL SERIES; *TNG*: THE NEXT GENERATION; *DS9*: DEEP SPACE NINE; *VOY*: VOYAGER; *ENT*: ENTERPRISE

Trek Universe

YOU NEED TO KNOW **BY COURTNEY MIFSUD**

ROMULAN

Planets: Romulus and Remus
Favorite tech: Cloaking device
Notables: Tomalak

Having renounced the Vulcan enlightenment, a splinter group formed what grew into the Romulan Star Empire. Political status and military duty are paramount in Romulan society, which warred against the Federation before an eventual peace treaty. The relationship remains filled with tension and mutual distrust.

Appeared in: *TOS, TNG, DS9, VOY, ENT*

BORG

Origin: Delta Quadrant
Power: Shared consciousness
Notables: Seven of Nine

Striving for a perfect society, the cybernetic Borg Collective operates by forcibly assimilating other species. The Borg grew into one of the most powerful species in the galaxy, conquering thousands of worlds. It would remain formidable until a war with Species 8472 allowed for the formation of a strong resistance movement.

Appeared in: *TNG, DS9, ENT, VOY*

BAJORAN

Planet: Bajor
Leader: A religious figure called the Kai
Notables: Kira Nerys, Ro Laren, Winn Adami

With a rich and spiritual ancestry, the Bajorans are rebuilding after a decades-long occupation of their planet by the Cardassian Union. The brutality of the occupation inspired a fierce Bajoran resistance movement. Eventually the Cardassians withdrew; a fragile Bajoran government partners with the Federation.

Appeared in: *TNG, DS9, VOY*

SPECIES 8472

Origin: Unknown
Weapon of choice: Infectious claws
Other power: Telepathic communication

Designated by the Borg Collective as Species 8472, the tripedal species resides in fluidic space, a separate dimension. Species 8472 is immune to the Borg's assimilation and proved to be its first concrete danger. With the Borg posing a mutual threat, *Voyager's* Capt. Janeway negotiated a tense cease-fire between Starfleet and Species 8472.

Appeared in: *VOY*

TRIBBLE

Planet: Iota Geminorum IV
Powers: Accelerated reproduction, tranquilizing sound emission

Non-sentient and small, a single Tribble might seem unthreatening. But give it enough food, and the born-pregnant fluffball will rapidly reproduce, birthing about 10 Tribbles per hour. While Tribbles emit a sound that soothes humans, they react violently to Klingons. Not ones to take a threat lightly, the Klingons set out to hunt down the Tribbles and destroy their home world.

Appeared in: *TOS, TNG, DS9, ENT*

TAKING KLINGON TO COURT

THE ALIEN LANGUAGE HAS SPARKED A VERY EARTHLY BATTLE

BY ALEX FITZPATRICK

WHO, IF ANYBODY, OWNS THE KLINGON language? That question, once the sole domain of extraordinarily geeky copyright scholars, has suddenly spilled into the fore—underscoring the surprisingly influential position of this made-up tongue.

It's all because of a legal battle over a *Star Trek* fan film called *Axanar*. *Axanar*'s creators have raised more than $600,000 from fellow Trekkers to make a feature-length movie set in the *Trek* universe. But they were sued by CBS and Paramount Pictures, which claim the rights to essentially all things *Trek*.

Heading into summer 2016, Paramount and CBS were said to be dropping the case—but not before one of their grievances set off a firestorm among *Trek* fans and legal experts. As part of the suit, the companies argued that the Klingon language, created by linguist Marc Okrand for 1984's *Star Trek III: The Search for Spock*, is among *Star Trek*'s copyrighted elements. That is no small claim.

Over the three decades since its creation, Klingon has morphed from a few lines uttered in a science-fiction franchise to a global phenomenon. Klingon is the most widely spoken fictional language in the world, according to *Guinness World Records*. There are multiple Klingon-to-English dictionaries, including a handy abridged version, *How to Speak Klingon: Essential Phrases for the Intergalactic Traveler*. Some of the most celebrated works of the English language, such as Shakespeare's *Hamlet*, have been translated into Klingon. A handful of die-hard fans even speak the language fluently, declaring *Qapla'!*, or "success," when they have achieved such mastery.

Devotees of fictional languages argue that if CBS and Paramount were afforded broad Klingon copyright protections, it could have a chilling effect on all that creativity—not to mention leave a sour taste in the mouths of *Trek*'s biggest fans. "Klingon, like any other spoken language, provides tools and a system for expressing ideas," reads an amicus brief filed in the case by the Language Creation Society, a nonprofit dedicated to "conlangs," or constructed languages. (The brief is, amusingly, dotted with Klingon expressions impossible to reproduce in the English alphabet of this terrestrial publication.) "No one has a monopoly over these things, effectively prohibiting anyone from communicating in a language without the creator's permission."

Marc Okrand, carrying his *Klingon Dictionary* (published in 1985), is carried by men dressed as Klingons at the National Air and Space Museum in 1992.

Indeed, some experts say that copyright law does not protect rules and processes such as languages. "My instinct, based on copyright doctrine, is that you cannot copyright the Klingon language as a whole," says Shyam Balganesh, a professor at the University of Pennsylvania Law School. Balganesh says the studios would have a more plausible case if *Axanar* had lifted specific Klingon dialogue from existing *Star Trek* TV episodes or films.

Whether a language enjoys copyright protection has implications even for those who may never read a Klingon version of *The Epic of Gilgamesh* (also available). A similar question was at the heart of Silicon Valley's fiercest legal battle so far this year. In the case, database firm Oracle accused Google of copyright infringement related to Java, an open-source programming language, in the process of building Android, Google's mobile operating system. It is well established that computer code written in a given language is protected by copyright. What has been less clear is the extent to which programming languages themselves enjoy the same protection, particularly when their source code is freely available (a status that makes them more analogous to spoken languages than to privately held code). Although Google won this particular battle, some technologists warn that the matter is far from settled—uncertainty that could have a chilling effect on technological innovation.

SPOCK AND AWE

THE DYNAMIC BETWEEN KIRK AND HIS VULCAN FIRST OFFICER RESULTED IN ONE OF SCIENCE FICTION'S MOST BELOVED ALIEN CHARACTERS

BY WILLIAM SHATNER

L EONARD NIMOY AND I CERTAINLY DIDN'T START OUR JOURNEY AS close friends. Rather, like the other members of our cast, we were colleagues, feeling each other out, learning our professional strengths and weaknesses and trying to bring our A game to the show. The friendships that developed initially were in the scripts: the relationship between Kirk and Spock held the show together. The two of us were onscreen in almost every scene. Leonard described the relationship between these two characters as a "great sense of brotherhood. Spock was tremendously loyal and had a great appreciation for the talent and the leadership abilities of Kirk. He was totally devoted to seeing to it that whatever Kirk needed to be done got done."

Conversely, Kirk relied on Spock unfailingly for his advice, knowing it would never be encumbered by any thoughts of personal gain or tempered by emotional constraints. But he also depended on him to share the burdens of command. With the exception of Dee Kelley's McCoy, Kirk had to maintain the distance of command from the rest of the crew. That can be a lonely place if there is no outlet, and Spock provided that outlet for Kirk.

Leonard Nimoy and William Shatner appear at a press conference for *Star Trek: The Motion Picture* in Los Angeles in 1979.

The first week we were on the air, there was one bag of mail. People were writing that they loved the show and asked for autographed pictures. That was encouraging. The second week we got three bags of mail. That was interesting. And then the deluge started, and in fact, it still hasn't ended. We had not the slightest idea what we were creating; we were always fighting to stay on the air one more season, one more week.

What was surprising to me was that rather than Capt. James T. Kirk, the character who received the most attention, and the most fan mail, was Mr. Spock. This was long before Leonard and I became friends, and honestly, I hadn't expected it, and I was not especially thrilled about it. I was being paid the largest salary, I was out front for the publicity, I had the most lines, my character's fate carried the story line, my character got the girl and saved the ship. The natural flow of events should have been that Kirk would receive the most attention, not some alien with strange-looking ears.

But the spectacular performance Leonard gave occupied all that attention in the beginning. Mr. Spock fan clubs were formed. Newspapers and magazines ran features on this extraordinary new character. Gene Roddenberry, the show's creator, got a memo from the network suggesting that Spock be featured in every story. My future was on the line, and that line seemed to be getting shaky. And so, for a few weeks, I was quite jealous. It bothered me so much that I went to Gene Roddenberry's office to discuss it with him. Gene was the voice of good reason in this case. "Don't be afraid of having other popular and talented people around you," he said. "They can only enhance your performance. The more you work with these people, the better the show is going to be." In other words, the more popular Spock became, the better it was for everyone, including me, and I settled down to that lovely fact.

Spock evolved as Leonard explored all the possibilities of the character. It was a considerably more complex task than usual because there were no recognizable hallmarks. This was a brand-new character in American culture; he was carving out the path. There was

no traditional right or wrong; the audience would tell him what was true. So Leonard took great care to protect Spock. He explained to me once, "No one else is going to provide that consistency and continuity. If the writers gave me the line 'Let's make hay under the Vulcan moon,' it was up to me to remind them that three episodes earlier Spock had mentioned that Vulcan had no moons."

Most of the hallmarks that became associated with Spock, in particular the Vulcan neck pinch and the Vulcan salute, were entirely Leonard's creation. In one of our first episodes, Kirk's personality was split into good and evil, and evil Kirk was about to kill good Kirk. In the script, Spock was supposed to sneak up behind evil Kirk and knock him out by hitting him over the head with the butt of his phaser. Leonard wasn't comfortable with that; brawling, banging someone in the head somehow seemed below Spock's evolved personality. It was too 20th-century. So he suggested to the director that Spock had a special capability that allowed him to put enemies out of action with little physical exertion. The director was

open to the concept.

Leonard and I sat down, and he told me what he had in mind: he would pinch my trapezius muscle, and I would collapse in a heap. I have no idea where that concept came from, but I was a professional actor; I knew how to fall down. Of course, it fit Spock perfectly: an advanced civilization would know where the vital nerves are located and have the physical strength to take advantage of that knowledge to incapacitate their enemy. We did the scene: Spock came up behind evil Kirk and pinched his trapezius, I dropped to the floor, and the Vulcan nerve pinch was born. For those people counting at home, fans of the show saw the Vulcan nerve pinch being used 34 different times. I wonder how many kids since then have had to suffer through the real pain of a Vulcan neck pinch.

OPPOSITES ATTRACT

As shipmates and friends, Kirk and Spock became one of the most memorable duos ever seen on TV—despite their many differences

——— ON LOVE ———

"Too much of anything . . . even love, isn't necessarily a good thing."
—Kirk, "The Trouble with Tribbles"

"After a time, you may find that having is not so pleasing a thing after all as wanting. It is not logical but is often true."
—Spock, "Amok Time"

——— ON WINNING ———

"I don't believe in the no-win scenario."
—Kirk, *Star Trek II: The Wrath of Khan*

"Vulcans never bluff."
—Spock, "The Doomsday Machine"

——— ON LOGIC ———

"Sometimes a feeling . . . is all we humans have to go on."
—Kirk, "A Taste of Armageddon"

"Logic is the beginning of wisdom . . . not the end."
—Spock, *Star Trek VI: The Undiscovered Country*

——— ON FUN ———

"The more complex the mind, the greater the need for the simplicity of play."
—Kirk, "Shore Leave"

"Humans smile with so little provocation."
—Spock, "Journey to Babel"

——— ON WAR ———

"It's instinctive. But the instinct can be fought."
—Kirk, "A Taste of Armageddon"

"Where there's no emotion, there's no motive for violence."
—Spock, "Dagger of the Mind"

The Vulcan salute has become recognized literally throughout the world. In this salute, the right hand is held up with the pinkie and ring finger touching but separated from the middle finger and forefinger, which also are touching, in a modified V-for-victory salute. It was created for the first episode of our second season, by which time Leonard had a strong understanding of Spock. In this episode, "Amok Time," Spock has to return to Vulcan to fulfill a marriage betrothal that was arranged when he was a child. If he doesn't return, he will die. This episode was written by the great science-fiction writer Theodore Sturgeon. This is the first time we have seen Spock on Vulcan, among the people of his race. In the script, he is greeted by the woman who is to conduct the marriage ceremony. Leonard suggested to the director that there needed to be some type of Vulcan greeting that would be appropriate. It would be the Vulcan version of a handshake, a kiss, a nod or bow, or a military salute. When the director agreed, Leonard had to create it. It was not an especially easy thing to envision. It needed to be unlike any traditional greeting, but it couldn't be at all comical. As he often did, Leonard drew on his own life to find it.

There is a gesture he had first seen when he was 8 years old, when he went with his grandfather, father and brother to an Orthodox synagogue, and he had never forgotten it. In Jewish Orthodox tradition, during the benediction, the Shechinah, which very roughly means the feminine counterpart to God, enters the sanctuary to bless the congregation. The Shechinah is so powerful that simply looking at it could cause serious or even fatal injury. So worshipers use this gesture, in which their fingers form the shape of the Hebrew letter *shin* to hide their eyes. The gesture always intrigued him. "I didn't know what it meant for a long time," he said. "But it seemed magical to me, and I learned how to do it." Not only did he use it as the basis for the traditional Vulcan greeting in the episode, many years later he published a controversial book of naked glamorous women wearing religious symbols, titled *Shekhina*. The gesture immediately caught on. Fans of the show started greeting him with it on the street—without realizing they were blessing each other.

Several of Spock's phrases also have become part of the general culture, but none of them are as widely known as the four words said when giving the Vulcan salute that have come to have such deep meaning: "Live long and prosper." They were written by Theodore Sturgeon for the same episode and are now known by the abbreviation LLAP—which was the way Leonard ended all his own tweets.

Spock eventually became a lasting archetype for an unemotional person. Even decades later, when *New York Times* columnist Maureen Dowd wanted to make the point that President Obama was dispassionate and distant, she referred to him as Spock. Spock's

SPOCK'S LACK OF EMOTION BECAME A CENTRAL THEME OF THE SHOW.

lack of emotion became a central theme of the show. In fact, a lot of the humor in the show came from the constant sparring between the very human Bones McCoy and Spock. In one episode, for example, Spock comments, "He reminds me of someone I knew in my youth." To which the surprised Bones responds, "Why, Spock, I didn't know you had one."

It is difficult for people who aren't actors to appreciate the talent it took to create a character that has become a part of American cultural history, the enigmatic Jay Gatsby of the 23rd century, destined to be played and interpreted by other actors. In less capable hands, it could have been a very one-dimensional role, but Leonard was able to create a dynamic inner life for Spock.

It resonated with audiences. Kids began wearing Spock ears, and Leonard received piles and piles of fan mail, far more than any of the other cast members. When he was out in public, people would greet him with a raised hand or wish him, "Live long and prosper." On a different level, I experienced the same thing. People began addressing me as "Captain" or "Kirk." That was a new experience for me. I'd had professional success, I'd played a role in some major movies, people recognized me, but I had never before been called by my character's name. It was odd, and in some ways, it made me uncomfortable. I'm not quite sure why, but it did. I wondered, What is that all about? It's crazy. So often I didn't acknowledge it, or I disparaged it.

Perhaps the strangest thing was that eventually Leonard became somewhat ambivalent about his relationship with Spock. Spock made Leonard's career. In each of the three years the show was on the air, Leonard was nominated for an Emmy for best supporting actor. *TV Guide* named Spock one of the 50 greatest characters in TV history. Leonard became well known and in demand because of the original series. But the new fear, replacing "I will never work again," was that he was so strongly identified as Spock that he could never escape him.

For someone who proudly described himself as a character actor, being so strongly typecast he could not play other roles was a terrifying possibility. His first autobiography, published in 1975, was titled *I Am Not Spock*. The title, he explained, came from a meeting in an airport in which a woman introduced him to her daughter as Spock—although the child was never convinced. It also came from the publisher's desire to profit from the popularity of Spock as well as create a little controversy. It was not, Leonard always insisted, meant to be a statement about his feelings about Spock, and he said if he ever had the opportunity to portray any fictional character, without hesitation he would choose Spock. And several years later, when he did write a second autobiography, it was titled *I Am Spock*. He had come full circle.

Adapted from Leonard, *by William Shatner with David Fisher. Copyright © 2016 by the authors and reprinted by permission of Thomas Dunne Books, an imprint of St. Martin's Press, LLC.*

A Shopping Spree

SURE, YOUR SPOCK LUNCH BOX WAS COOL. BUT MARKETERS HAVE BEEN

For the lifelong Trekker: a photon-torpedo-style casket.

Spock beamed into Burger King (in toy form) to promote the 2009 *Star Trek* movie.

Romulan Ale was sold at the now-shuttered Star Trek: The Experience in Las Vegas.

It turns out that the *Enterprise* design makes for an effective pizza cutter too.

This tri-dimensional chess set lets you play the game Kirk and Spock loved.

Starfleet swimmers can command the pool from this inflatable captain's-chair float.

at the Final Frontier

TURNING OUT NEW *TREK* MERCHANDISE AT WARP SPEED **BY COURTNEY MIFSUD**

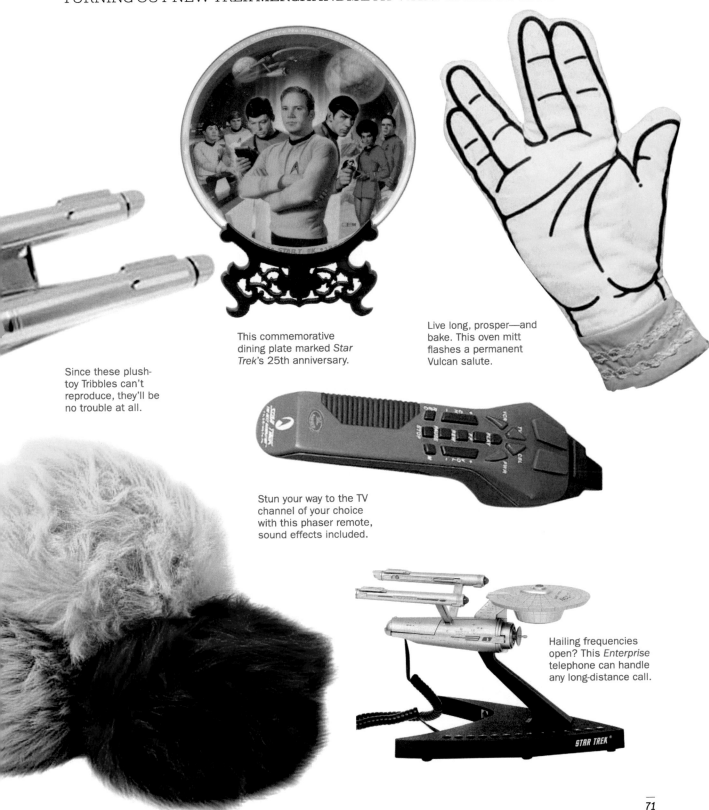

This commemorative dining plate marked *Star Trek*'s 25th anniversary.

Live long, prosper—and bake. This oven mitt flashes a permanent Vulcan salute.

Since these plush-toy Tribbles can't reproduce, they'll be no trouble at all.

Stun your way to the TV channel of your choice with this phaser remote, sound effects included.

Hailing frequencies open? This *Enterprise* telephone can handle any long-distance call.

Star Trek  VS.

IT'S THE ULTIMATE FAN ARGUMENT: WHICH IS BETTER? PARTISAN FEELINGS RUN DEEP ON BOTH SIDES, BUT IN HONOR OF *TREK*'S 50TH ANNIVERSARY, *TIME*'S EDITORS SIZED

THE FLAGSHIP

U.S.S. Enterprise **vs.**

Millennium Falcon

The U.S.S. *Enterprise*, in all of its incarnations, is a futuristic aircraft carrier, conveying hundreds of crew members and projecting Federation power while also exploring new worlds. Han Solo's ship, in contrast, is more like the SUV of space vessels: a rugged and (mostly) reliable transport for a small band.

Winner: *Star Trek*

Here's why:
The *Falcon* may have famously made the Kessel Run in "less than 12 parsecs," but the basic design of the *Enterprise*— with its saucer section and two engine nacelles—has remained iconic for more than 50 years.

THE ENEMY

Borg Cube **vs.**

Death Star

Both are fearsome combatants. Redundant technology on a Borg ship allows it to absorb massive amounts of damage and still function. On the Death Star, technology seems to function well, though the middle managers who run the station have repeatedly proved incompetent.

Winner: *Star Wars*

Here's why:
A Borg Cube can slice a section out of an opponent's ship, but the Death Star has enough firepower to blow up an entire planet.

HAND WEAPON

Phaser **vs.**

Lightsaber

Phasers are mass-produced weapons that pack a lot of punch in a small package— they can even be programmed to overload as an improvised grenade. The lightsaber is, as Obi-Wan Kenobi described it, "an elegant weapon," and it can also deflect shots from blasters (the phasers of the *Star Trek* universe).

Winner: TIE

Here's why:
A phaser offers more utility, since it can stun or kill an opponent or just heat rocks to keep you warm, but a lightsaber looks good, sounds good and instantly signals your strength with the Force.

THE ANDROID

Data **vs.**

C-3PO

Data, a human-looking android, is a key trusted crew member in *Star Trek: The Next Generation*. He has even commanded a starship in combat. Threepio is much shinier—and often forced to serve as comic relief in the *Star Wars* universe.

Winner: *Star Trek*

Here's why:
Data has become a beloved character both for his persistence in trying to become more human and for fighting for equal rights for artificial life-forms (unlike a certain subservient protocol droid).

CUDDLY CHARACTERS

Tribbles **vs.**

Ewoks

Although they're soft and furry, fast-breeding Tribbles don't look particularly cute— but their purring is known to have a powerfully soothing effect on humans. Ewoks, who are native to the forest moon of Endor, are essentially sentient teddy bears.

Winner: *Star Wars*

Here's why:
The Ewoks are indisputably adorable, but they also rock as allies in battle, improvising weapons and traps to defeat adversaries.

Star Wars

UP THE RIVALRY IN 10 KEY CATEGORIES.
HERE'S OUR COMPLETELY IMPARTIAL GUIDE
TO THE GALAXY'S GREATEST DEBATE

POLITICAL SYSTEM

United Federation of Planets

 vs.

The Empire

It's not entirely clear how *Star Trek*'s Federation is governed, but it appears to be essentially democratic. Its high ideals—including a non-interference Prime Directive— make it a good neighbor. The Empire of *Star Wars*, despite having roots in a more democratic republic, exercises brutal control over its territory.

Winner: *Star Trek*

Here's why:
The Federation generally keeps the peace and respects diversity but doesn't shrink from a fight when threatened.

EXPENDABLE CHARACTERS

Redshirts

 vs.

Stormtroopers

It appears no space fleet can get by without cannon fodder. *Trek*'s crimson-shirted officers have such a brief life expectancy that the term "redshirt" is now used generically for characters who die shortly after their first appearance. But work conditions are even worse for stormtroopers, who seem to have galactically bad aim in firefights.

Winner: *Star Trek*

Here's why:
The trope of the clueless redshirt has become a reliable—and cherished—aspect of fandom.

HAIRSTYLE (MEN'S)

Spock

 vs.

Han Solo

To be fair to Han Solo, it was the 1970s. Mussed and a little shaggy was sexy—and easy to care for when on the run from Jabba the Hutt. Though most men in the original *Trek* series seemed to have pointed sideburns, Spock paired his with an achingly precise style that showed off his pointed ears and slanted eyebrows.

Winner: *Star Trek*

Here's why:
Han's look says "scoundrel" (the good kind), but Spock's hair is instantly recognizable—even to earthlings.

HAIRSTYLE (WOMEN'S)

Yeoman Rand

 vs.

Princess Leia

To be fair to Yeoman Rand and her beehive coiffure, she was appearing on a TV show smack in the 1960s, which spanned mod looks to hippie fashions. Leia's coiled-bun hairdo, meanwhile, was a true original.

Winner: *Star Wars*

Here's why:
Which look would you rather sport at a costume party?

BEST BAR

Ten-Forward

 vs.

The Mos Eisley cantina

The most notable bar in *Star Trek* is *Next Generation*'s Ten-Forward, a sleek and mostly sedate space overseen by Guinan (Whoopi Goldberg), bartender and unofficial counselor. To grab a drink in *Star Wars*, head to the iconic Mos Eisley cantina on Tatooine, also a great place to hire a mercenary ship.

Winner: *Star Wars*

Here's why:
Mos Eisley may be a "wretched hive of scum and villainy," as Obi-Wan Kenobi put it, but the music is great—and the staff won't try to serve you synthehol, Starfleet's alcohol substitute.

RISE OF THE TREKKER

THE ORIGINAL SERIES WAS CANCELED AFTER THREE SEASONS, BUT IT CREATED A LEGION OF PASSIONATE FANS WHO HAVE RESHAPED POPULAR CULTURE

BY REED TUCKER

"G ET A LIFE!" WILLIAM SHATNER FAMOUSLY ADMONISHED A stunned group of *Star Trek* fans in a 1986 *Saturday Night Live* sketch. "You've turned an enjoyable little job that I did as a lark for a few years into a colossal waste of time." The skit hit the cultural bull's-eye—Shatner even called his 1999 memoir *Get a Life!*—because it perfectly played into the pervasive stereotype of *Trek* fans as antisocial losers living in their mothers' basements.

"It's just a TV show, damn it," Shatner pleaded. "It's just a TV show."

Turns out it wasn't, and it isn't.

It has now become clear that those long-mocked Trekkers are among the most influential groups in entertainment history. That tight little band of fanatics who rallied around the original series starting back in 1966 basically paved the way for so much of what we see in pop culture today as well as pioneered the manner in which so many of us consume it. That guy wearing the plastic ears and phaser holster? He's now the mainstream.

"*Star Trek* really started it all," says Daryl Frazetti, a Western Nevada College professor who's taught classes on the franchise. "They were the first to bring the mythology to the fans and allow them to participate in parts of that myth."

When *Trek* premiered on Sept. 8, 1966, on NBC, viewers could sense they had something different. Networks had aired science-

Fans of the series from Long Island, N.Y., sport homemade headgear at a 1976 convention at the Statler Hilton Hotel in Manhattan.

fiction shows before, but many, such as *Lost in Space* and *Captain Video and His Video Rangers*, were aimed at younger viewers. With *Star Trek*, creator Gene Roddenberry offered a more intelligent spin on the future. Here was a series that often subordinated action and explosions in favor of character-driven stories that provided veiled commentary on the touchiest social issues of '60s-era America, including racism, religion and militarism.

"In the mid-'60s, prime-time TV was coming out of this western phase and transitioning into the escapist sitcom era, where you get *Mr. Ed* and *I Dream of Jeannie*," says Arthur Smith, an assistant curator at the Paley Center for Media. "*Star Trek* looked like a juvenile serial, but it was very adult and serious in its aims. It was absolutely different for that time."

Viewers noticed, and a fan base quickly grew around the show. With just three networks on the dial in that era, programming was designed to appeal to as wide an audience as possible, and in that respect, *Star Trek* failed. The series sputtered in the ratings and was canceled after just three seasons. Back then, TV ratings and viewing demographics weren't nearly as sophisticated as they are

Bjo and John Trimble are famous Trekkers who campaigned for the naming of the shuttle *Enterprise* and even appeared in *Star Trek: The Motion Picture*.

today, but it was clear from the limited data gathered that what the *Trek* audience lacked in size, it made up for in passion. "The audience was small, but it was incredibly consistent," Smith says. "It was a dedicated audience."

At the time, no one could have guessed how dedicated. Through the series's run and in the years following the show's cancellation, Trekkers pioneered a more active and extreme type of participation with the franchise they loved. Fan fiction? Conventions? Dressing in costumes for "cosplay"? Sound familiar?

"It really set the stage for everything that's happening now in fandom," says Marc Cushman, a former *Star Trek: The Next Generation* writer and the author of *These Are the Voyages*, a close look at the original series. "The networks and the studios didn't think anyone took shows seriously. They viewed TV as disposable."

At the time, television was generally a passive activity. Programs were things to be received while sitting on the couch, and that's where

the interaction generally began and ended. *Star Trek* watchers, however, wanted more from the experience—a stronger, deeper interaction with the franchise. They wanted more ownership, and that same desire forms the basis for hard-core fandom today, whether it's Pottermaniacs, Twihards or Marvel zombies.

The Trekkers grew out of the disparate print science-fiction community that had existed since the 1930s, borrowing some of its practices and traditions. When the show was threatened with cancellation after its second season, fans mobilized to save it. Two avid viewers, husband and wife John and Bjo Trimble, heard a rumor while on a set visit that *Trek* was getting axed. On the way home, they formulated a plan to change the network's mind by rallying thousands of fans to write letters in support. A group of science-fiction writers led by Harlan Ellison had deployed a similar tactic following season one.

"It was entirely a grassroots thing," says Bjo Trimble, now 82. "We did this all by mail. We contacted fans from all over the United States."

The couple got in touch with Roddenberry, and he provided addresses from fans who

College students demonstrate outside NBC Studios in Burbank, Calif., in response to rumors of the show's cancellation in early 1968.

had written to the show. The Trimbles also procured a sci-fi-convention mailing list and a list from a book dealer. (Despite rumors, the Trimbles insist Roddenberry was not behind the Save Trek campaign.) It wasn't the first TV letter-writing campaign, but it's arguably the best-known, and it cemented the idea in viewers' heads that their voices mattered.

"If thousands of fans just sit around moaning about the death of *Star Trek*, they will get exactly what they deserve: *GOMER PYLE!* (Yetch!)," the Trimbles wrote in 1967. "So pass the word, and write some letters, people; it's up to us fans to keep *Star Trek* on TV."

NBC was reportedly deluged with some 100,000 missives. The flood of mail was so deep, the network apparently had trouble dealing with it all. It later took the unusual step of announcing on air that *Trek* would "continue to be seen on NBC Television." In other words: if you would be so kind, stop writing us these letters.

Besides the fan base's passion, the letters also proved something else. "The network had told Roddenberry that *Star Trek* viewers were a bunch of sci-fi kooks and kids," Cushman says. "Then they found out, no, these people worked for NASA. They were college students and professors. The fans crossed all avenues."

Such an educated audience knew its stuff, so the makers of *Star Trek* vetted scripts with real-world science experts to ensure that the technology and scenarios were plausible (if not probable). Compare that with today, when noted astrophysicist Neil deGrasse Tyson takes to Twitter to point out inconsistencies in the film *Interstellar* and dozens of publications present fact checks of Sandra Bullock's *Gravity*.

Viewers of *Trek* did seem to take the show more seriously than those of, say, *The Hollywood Squares*. One trivial innovation Trekkers can claim is the first use of the now-ubiquitous term "spoiler alert." The expression initially cropped up in a 1982 Usenet newsgroup discussion of *Star Trek II: The Wrath of Khan*, according to the *Wall Street Journal*, and was designed to shield the uninformed from the potentially life-altering revelation that (spoiler alert) Spock dies.

ANOTHER ADVANCE THE FRANCHISE MADE was in merchandising. Do you know a child clamoring for a $150 Lego *Millennium Falcon*? You can probably thank—or curse—*Star Trek*.

In 1967, with the help of the Trimbles, Roddenberry launched Lincoln Enterprises, a mail-order company selling show merch.

"The fans wanted just about anything with *Star Trek*," John Trimble says. "Gene had been noodling about in his mind about doing a merchandise company, but he knew nothing about running a mail-order company. Bjo and I had run a few."

Some tie-ins, including a comic book and a board game, were already in stores, but the idea that fans would want (and pay) more was novel at the time. "Paramount [the studio] had no clue what they were doing with *Star Trek*," Bjo Trimble says. "They put out a chalkboard for kids with the *Enterprise* upside down. It was just stuff they slapped STAR TREK on." Paramount was so lukewarm on the prospect of merchandising that the studio allowed Da-

New York, 1974

London, 1994

Atlanta, 2002

San Diego, 2013

Frankfurt, 2014

Trekkers have been convening at locations around the world since the 1970s. The gatherings typically include autograph signings, merchandise sales and, of course, costumed attendees.

vid Gerrold, the writer behind the episode "The Trouble with Tribbles," to sell replicas of the furry creatures.

Lincoln was set up to offer an insider merchandise experience. The company began offering shirt insignias, scripts and bits of discarded film from the show. Fans could literally own a piece of *Trek*. "No other show has ever made an offer like this!!!" the catalog trumpeted.

"Roddenberry was making a lot of money," Cushman says. "That woke the industry up. They realized these people love the show and it's a way of life for them. This changed everything as far as how studios saw the fans."

In one shrewd bit of product placement, Roddenberry rewrote a script to include a "pointless" speech praising a medallion so that a replica could later be sold, according to Shatner's autobiography. "If you're looking around for more things to merchandise and you have the right to write it into a script, why not?" asks Bjo Trimble.

What was also novel about *Trek*'s merchandise empire is that most of it was built after the show went off the air. The series famously found a second wind in reruns, becoming one of the first shows to have a life beyond its initial prime-time slot. According to legend, it has run continuously on some station in the world ever since it was canned in 1969. Modern Hollywood, where no franchise ever goes away and no pre-sold property, no matter how dusty, is unfit for exploitation (*A-Team* movie, anyone?), owes plenty to *Trek*.

The series was an unusual candidate for syndication, in part because it was never a ratings hit, but also because it produced only 79 episodes, not the 100 traditionally required for reruns. In the end, that limited number might have been a boon to fans and helped usher in another facet of modern pop culture: Ph.D.-thesis-level immersion.

"A smaller number of episodes meant the episodes were rerun more frequently," Smith says. "You'd think viewers would get burned out. Counterintuitively, it became this almost Talmudic study of the *Star Trek* universe. On the ninth time around, you've parsed every line of dialogue, analyzed every behind-the-scenes political situation. It was an opportu-

Enthusiastic Trekkers, many donning *Enterprise* uniforms, gather at a 2011 convention at the Rio Hotel and Casino in Las Vegas.

nity to amass this lore and really become an expert on this thing." A few years later, the success of *Star Wars*—and so many of the blockbusters that followed—would be driven largely by repeat viewings. Three months after *A New Hope* opened, purportedly 4 in 10 viewers had already seen it twice or more.

Perhaps the only drawback to having just 79 *Trek* episodes was that it left some viewers wanting more. Desperate for new material, they ultimately took matters into their hands and began exploring their beloved series in more personal ways. The first *Trek*-focused fanzine, *Spockanalia*, appeared in 1967. It was 90 pages, mimeographed and produced by fans Devra Langsam and Sherna Comerford. It contained a letter from Leonard Nimoy and various articles, as well as a poem by Dorothy Jones titled "The Territory of Rigel." It read, in part, "On the bridge am I, silence upon silence, as quiet as memory, and dark as death." *Spockanalia* is also notable for containing several amateur-written *Trek* stories; it's considered the birthplace of fan fiction.

"Fan fiction introduced the idea that a TV series was not the definitive text in a franchise," Smith says. "It's a rich enough world to transcend its original TV setting. We've seen that with *The X-Files* and other shows."

For the first time, a fan's contribution to a show's canon was seen as worthwhile and as valid as what was on the air, and that revolutionary idea has transformed entertainment. The superhero movies that now dominate the multiplexes, for example, owe a debt to this blurring of the line between fan and professional. Some of these films are based on stories written by former "letterhacks"—fans known for writing letters to comics publishers—who broke into Marvel and DC in the 1970s, and they're directed by former fanboys, such as Zack Snyder. And what was *Star Wars: The Force Awakens* besides expensive fan fiction bankrolled by Disney?

One particular strain of *Trek* fan-fic proved especially influential: slash. The genre grew out of viewers' imaginings of what would happen if Spock beamed into Kirk's bedroom. The first of these romantic tales, "A Fragment out of Time," by Diane Marchant, appeared in 1974, and the practice soon spread to other fandoms. Slash was written almost exclusively by women, for women.

Today, the Internet is awash in massive

slash depositories fantasizing about the bedroom habits of everyone from *Game of Thrones* wildlings to, disturbingly, Bambi. The genre has also earned millions for *Fifty Shades of Grey* creator E.L. James and turned other armchair authors into hot publishing commodities.

NOT THAT WE'RE JUDGING. IN FACT, ONE OF the hallmarks of a *Trek* fan is that he or she is accepting of all kinds of people, no matter the race, gender or ear shape. The program posited a future in which a starship would be staffed by a diverse crew, and it famously presented one of TV's first interracial kisses.

"The show set a tone and appealed to the kind of people who were willing to accept 'infinite diversity in infinite combinations,'" says

A TREK *FAN IS* ACCEPTING OF ALL KINDS, NO MATTER THE RACE, GENDER OR EAR SHAPE.

John Trimble, referring to a Vulcan philosophy featured on the show. "That was implicit in the show. Fans picked up on that and acted on it."

The world is only now catching up with that attitude, and inclusiveness is becoming a priority in pop culture. Fans demand a gay *Star Wars* character and lament the lack of woman-led superhero flicks. The original series fandom was unusually diverse, welcoming women, people of color and the physically challenged, helping to lay the groundwork for a world in which someone can attend the midnight premiere of *The Hobbit* dressed in a homemade, $3,000 orc costume and fellow ticket buyers barely look up from their iPhones.

Or a world where 100,000-plus can gather at San Diego Comic-Con with nary a harsh word said nor phaser drawn. That proliferation of pop-culture conventions today partly traces its roots to Kirk and company. The first *Star Trek* convention opened its doors on

Jan. 21, 1972, in New York City. Enthusiasts had organized generalized science-fiction and comic-book conventions before, but that con is considered the first dedicated to a specific media property. It drew some 3,000 Trekkers.

"Without the influence of *Star Trek*, we wouldn't have this industry," says Zachery McGinnis, an appearance agent who books talent at genre conventions. He's worked with George Takei and Walter Koenig. "Every weekend there are multiple events around the world—Guatemala, Australia, Peru. There are endless amounts of events now."

Not to mention seemingly endless ways to commune with the franchise. *Trek*'s modern-day resurrection began back in the 1970s when an executive at Paramount's parent company saw the success of *Star Wars* and phoned another suit, asking, "Don't we own something like that?" *Star Trek: The Motion Picture*, released in 1979, became one of the first TV programs adapted for the big screen, demonstrating once again that defunct franchises could live on in other ways. Critics weren't kind, but the movie was successful enough to spawn multiple sequels and four spinoff TV series.

A rebooted *Star Trek*, directed by J.J. Abrams, warped into theaters in 2009. The film edged closer to traditional summer blockbusters in its tone, and to many *Trek* purists, it felt like a betrayal of the property's roots. Two sequels followed, including the summer 2016 film *Star Trek Beyond*. And while some superfans are not impressed ("We thought the movies were very disappointing," Bjo Trimble says), others are happy to keep *Star Trek*'s mission going.

"The good thing about the [2009] film, it revitalized the franchise and brought in a lot of new fans," says the anthropologist Frazetti, who saw it seven times in the theater. "You had people who'd never even looked at *Star Trek* and thought we [Trekkers] were crazy, who saw these films and loved them and have now entered into fandom."

Shatner was wrong. These people don't need to get a life. The rest of us have gotten theirs.

Reed Tucker is a New York City journalist who writes about culture and entertainment.

FAMOUS FANS

SCIENTISTS, MOVIE STARS, WORLD LEADERS: EVERYBODY LOVES *STAR TREK*

BY COURTNEY MIFSUD

ANGELINA JOLIE

The actress and director told Jon Stewart in 1999 that her crush on Spock came from the character's restraint: "I was focused on Spock . . . he was so repressed, and I just wanted to make him scream."

STEPHEN HAWKING

Not only is *Star Trek* Stephen Hawking's favorite show, but the physicist and author made a 1993 cameo appearance (as a holographic poker partner for Data).

COLIN POWELL

When *The Next Generation* had an episode in which Wesley Crusher was promoted to full ensign, Gene Roddenberry gave actor Wil Wheaton Roddenberry's own rank insignia from his World War II service. Future secretary of state Colin Powell, then chairman of the joint chiefs, visited the set for the occasion and sat in Capt. Picard's chair.

BARACK OBAMA

The 44th president declared, "I loved Spock," when he paid tribute to Leonard Nimoy in 2015. The pair had met at an event with presidential candidates in 2007. Obama's calm, analytical demeanor has caused some to liken him to Spock.

ROSARIO DAWSON

Dawson taught Conan O'Brien some Klingon when she appeared on his show in 2010. *"Qapla'!"* the actress and activist declared, uttering the Klingon word for "success."

MAYA ANGELOU

"I loved *Star Trek*," author Maya Angelou told TIME in 2013. Angelou, who died in 2014, said she was drawn to the show by the presence of her friend, actor Nichelle Nichols, who played Lt. Uhura.

NEIL DEGRASSE TYSON

Partial to the original 1960s version, the astrophysicist weighed in on the *Trek*-versus-*Wars* debate. Choose between the *Enterprise* and the *Millennium Falcon*? "Oh, that's easy! . . . The *Enterprise*—there's no question."

RICHARD BRANSON

The English business mogul and Virgin Group founder renamed Virgin Galactic's SpaceShipTwo as the V.S.S. *Enterprise*, an homage to *Star Trek*'s flagship vessel.

TOM HANKS

The Oscar-winning actor challenged *Star Trek*'s Simon Pegg (Scotty) to a *Trek* trivia contest on *The Graham Norton Show* in 2011. Hanks held his own and explained that his entire family shares his love of *Trek*.

THE DALAI LAMA

In the early 1990s a delegation of the Dalai Lama's Tibetan monks visited a *Star Trek* set. The Dalai Lama had watched *Star Trek* in the past and was fond of "the man with big ears."

A POLITICAL ENTERPRISE

FROM VIETNAM IN THE 1960S TO MORE RECENT DEBATES ABOUT TORTURE AND TERRORISM, EACH *STAR TREK* SERIES CHARTED A COLLISION COURSE WITH SOCIAL ISSUES

BY SUSANNA SCHROBSDORFF

ONSIDER THIS AMAZING FACT: A SHOW THAT BEGAN 50 YEARS ago as a sci-fi fantasy with embarrassingly cheap sets, awkward fight scenes and some very bad wigs turned out to be an enduring platform for serious political and social commentary. From racism to the ethics of global interventionism, *Star Trek* took on topics that seemed untouchable and beamed them right into prime time, all lightly disguised in alien makeup.

Sure, there were certain episodes in the original series of the 1960s that didn't slip under the radar, like the one with that famous Kirk-Uhura interracial kiss. But as *Star Trek* has been reincarnated decade after decade, it has continued to both reflect its times and challenge them, slyly poking at the most tender and divisive issues in American culture.

The early politics of the show were driven by creator Gene Roddenberry's vision of a future in which humans have evolved to the point where all races can live together and there is no war. For a country with vivid memories of World War II and worries about

In "A Private Little War" (1968), the *Enterprise* crew find that the planet Neural, home to a primitive society, is being supplied with weapons by the Klingons.

the nuclear threat, *Star Trek* was the ultimate escape—a small-screen view of the furthest reaches of President John F. Kennedy's New Frontier. "It showed you what the world might look like in 400 years if you were in some kind of fantasy," says William Shatner, who played Capt. James T. Kirk.

The bridge of the U.S.S. *Enterprise* reflected that fantasy. Roddenberry was a vet and had been a pilot in the Pacific theater, where the United States had engaged in horrific battles with Japanese forces. But on the *Enterprise*, that animosity was long healed; to

THE BATTLES THE MULTICULTURAL CREW FACED IN SPACE WERE ROOTED IN THE CONFLICTS OF THE TIME.

prove it, Roddenberry put a Japanese American, George Takei, on the bridge as Lt. Sulu. Takei and his family had been in an American internment camp during the war, making his presence even more poignant.

In the real world of the '60s, the conflict between the U.S. and the Soviet Union was heating up, but Roddenberry's crew dared to add a Russian officer, Pavel Chekov (Walter Koenig). And as civil rights battles spilled into America's streets and played out on everyone's television screens, Roddenberry cast an African-American woman, Nichelle Nichols, as communications officer Lt. Uhura. At the time, just having a woman on the bridge of a (quasi-)military vessel was a bit transgressive; a black woman was revolutionary. Then there was Leonard Nimoy's Spock, an officer of mixed race (half Vulcan, half human)—which was also a subversive concept at the time.

RODDENBERRY'S MULTICULTURAL CREW MAY have been a symbol of a harmonious future,

but the battles they faced in space were rooted in the conflicts of the time. "*Star Trek* directly reflected the politics of the Kennedy era and the Cold War," says Paul Cantor, a professor of English at the University of Virginia and a *Star Trek* scholar. "Fundamentally the United Federation of Planets was the United States," he says. "The Klingons were Russians and militaristic, while the Federation stood for democracy and liberalism."

The core of Roddenberry's moral universe was the Prime Directive, a standing order that forbids Starfleet personnel from interfering with other cultures—even if the goal is to help. From the start, it was a rule meant to be broken, or at least debated. That tension was central to the show, says Shatner. "When does the intuitive conscience of man take precedence over the written law? When do you interfere, and when do you not interfere? It's a question that's been asked a lot in politics," he says. "And in our case, in *Star Trek*, it added to the drama of an individual flying in the face of bureaucracy."

In fact, Kirk seemed to be constantly violating the Prime Directive. "It became a bit of a joke," says Cantor. "Every episode is about interference in some planet. And what it came down to is that we don't interfere in another planet, provided it looks exactly like Kennedy's 1960s America."

This idea that America was both the protector of freedom and the standard by which other countries should be judged permeated the original *Star Trek*. The tone had been set by Kennedy's landmark 1961 inaugural speech, which was practically a mandate for intervention. The U.S. would, Kennedy said, "pay any price, bear any burden, meet any hardship, support any friend, oppose any foe to assure the survival and the success of liberty."

That's the real directive Kirk seemed to be following. Timothy Sandefur, an adjunct scholar at the Cato Institute and a *Star Trek* fan, points out that the show once went so far as to have Kirk rapturously recite the pre-

---

→

John F. Kennedy's 1961 inaugural promise that the U.S. would "bear any burden, meet any hardship, support any friend, oppose any foe to assure the survival and the success of liberty" was regularly echoed in the plots and themes of the 1960s series.

amble to the Constitution. In that episode, "The Omega Glory," two races are at war: the "Yangs" (yankees) and the "Kohms" (communists), who represent the Americans and the Chinese. But the Yangs have become savages. They've forgotten the values imbued in the tattered American flag and the crumbling copy of the Constitution that they worship. Kirk steps in to set things right, and when First Officer Spock objects, he explains, "We merely showed them the meaning of what they were fighting for. Liberty and freedom have to be more than just words."

Another episode evoked the liberation of the death camps in World War II. In "A Taste of Armageddon," the *Enterprise* crew discover a planet that has been in a civil war for decades—but fighting only by computer. There are no bombs, and civilization is not destroyed. Instead, when one side suffers damages in a computerized "attack," it must execute a commensurate number of citizens. Kirk is unable to let this systemized slaughter continue, and he intervenes. "We don't make war with computers and herd the casualties into suicide stations," he says before blowing up the death machines.

Shatner suggests that "Armageddon" foreshadows modern warfare, with its drones and remote-controlled bombs. "It's a war by computer where the nations had lost sight of how horrible war is," he says. "It has ramifications, particularly now. What was science fiction then has become science fact now. But what remains is the human confusion, the human chaos of what to do and how to do it."

Toward the end of the original series, the threshold for intervention seemed less clear. By 1968, casualties were mounting in Vietnam and young people were protesting the draft. "A Private Little War" was an overt allegory of America's involvement in the conflict. In

In "The Omega Glory" (1968), Kirk cites the U.S. Constitution: "Look at these three words . . . tall words proudly saying, 'We the People.'"

it, a peaceful but primitive people get caught between two superpowers. Kirk discovers that some of them have been armed with rifles by the Klingons. Kirk, after some debate, decides to give weapons to the other side. His rationale is a Cold War primer: "A balance of power. The trickiest, most difficult, dirtiest game of them all, but the only one that preserves both sides."

Perhaps the most powerful political statement made by any *Star Trek* episode in any era was that of "Let That Be Your Last Battlefield," which took on racism. The *Enterprise* beams up two alien survivors of a long war. One of them is black on the right side of his face and white on the other side. The second alien has the reverse pattern. And they despise each other as a result. Once aboard, the two try to kill each other, causing chaos. They are returned to their planet, where presumably they live out their lives in hate.

The episode aired in 1969, the year after Martin Luther King Jr. was assassinated and not long before the series was canceled. It is one of Shatner's favorites. "That was such a brilliant concept," he says. "I'd never seen that before and never seen it done again as brilliantly, imaginatively showing us the ignorance and the stupidity of racism." It was written by Gene Coon, another military vet, who produced 33 episodes and whom Shatner describes as "the real generator of the success of *Star Trek*."

IF 1960S *TREK* WAS ALL ABOUT BEING A HERO, then *Star Trek: The Next Generation*, which premiered in 1987, portrayed a more complicated moral universe. "You start off in the first *Star Trek*, and the Earth is effectively the center of the universe, of everything," explains Paul Cantor. But when *Next Generation* debuted, the Iron Curtain was about to fall, the Cold War was ending, and a polarized view of the world was beginning to dissolve. "This is

when you first get a sense [in the series] that there are forces out there that may be superior, whole civilizations that may be more advanced," says Cantor.

Unlike Kirk, the new captain of the *Enterprise*, Jean-Luc Picard, is not a classic American hero. He's not even American; he's French. And he's played by British actor Patrick Stewart. Picard has a different interpretation of the Prime Directive. When the *Enterprise* discovers a race that is keeping people on a nearby planet addicted to a drug to enslave them, the ship's medical officer, Beverly Crusher (Gates McFadden), begs Picard to help. Picard declines: "It is not for me to make any of these decisions," he says. "The Prime Directive is not just a set of rules; it is a philosophy . . . and a very correct one." Picard reflects post-Vietnam America's skittishness when he adds, "History has proved again and again that whenever mankind interferes with a less developed civilization, no matter how well-intentioned that interference may be, the results are invariably disastrous."

Timothy Sandefur sees Picard's reluctance to get involved as a shift from Roddenberry's original vision: "In *The Next Generation*, the Prime Directive becomes a dogma based on moral and cultural relativism, symptomatic of the Clinton era. That continued until September 11. Since then, the idea that there is such a thing as genuine evil has seen a resurgence among liberal intellectuals."

Still, *TNG* broke some political ground. *Star Trek* had long been criticized for not having a recurring gay character. But Jeri Taylor, a writer and executive producer on the series, addressed homosexuality in at least one episode. In "The Outcast," a race of androgynous beings has banned all identifications of male or female gender. When one of the beings comes out as female, she's threatened with a kind of sexual re-education. Taylor says it would have been difficult to broach homophobia at the time other than through science fiction. "It allowed the freedom to talk about bias

and intolerance in a way that would be much harder for people to hear if it were presented in a contemporary context," she says.

The Next Generation was eerily prescient about some ethical questions that continue to this day. The most searing example is probably the 1992 episode "Chain of Command." Written years before the invasion of Iraq, it echoes some of the excruciating debates about torture Americans would have after 9/11. The story has Picard captured by the Cardassians, a hostile race developing biological weapons of mass destruction. Picard protests his treat-

TNG *WAS PRESCIENT ABOUT SOME ETHICAL QUESTIONS THAT CONTINUE TO THIS DAY.*

ment, saying he's protected as a prisoner of war under a 24th-century analogue of the Geneva Conventions, but the Cardassians use a loophole in the definition of "prisoner of war" and leave the captain naked and strung up by the wrists all night.

The next day, the chief torturer shines four lights in Picard's eyes repeatedly, and, using a remote control that applies pain, he insists that Picard say there are five lights. Picard resists, taunting his captor: "Torture has never been a reliable means of extracting information. It is ultimately self-defeating as a means of control. One wonders that it's still practiced." Just before Picard collapses entirely, his crewmates negotiate his release. Later, Picard tells the ship's counselor that he did not break, but he admits he would have if he hadn't been rescued. He says he would have said anything to get relief. And he adds, "But more than that, I believed that I could see five lights."

ANOTHER POLITICAL ISSUE THAT SURFACED IN 1990s *Star Trek* and still runs hot today is income disparity. *Deep Space Nine*, a spinoff

In *The Next Generation*'s "Chain of Command, Part II" (1992), Picard (right) protests his torture by his captors, citing an agreement governing treatment of prisoners of war.

about a Federation outpost that guards the opening of a wormhole, debuted in 1993 with the series's first African-American lead, Avery Brooks, as Cdr. Benjamin Sisko. In "Past Tense," Sisko and two crew members, Julian Bashir (Alexander Siddig) and Jadzia Dax (Terry Farrell), accidentally end up in San Francisco circa 2024. At that time, the country's jobless "gimmes" and the mentally ill "dims" were segregated into "Sanctuary Districts," similar to debtors' prisons. Outside, the wealthy live undisturbed by the desperation in the camps. But a violent revolution causes the public to turn against the slums and finally deal with poverty and homelessness.

When this episode aired in 1995, the U.S. was conflicted over a welfare-reform bill (enacted in 1996) that pushed "personal responsibility" and cut aid. The debate flared up again in the 2016 presidential primaries when Social Democrat Bernie Sanders ignited a populist movement against entrenched economic inequality.

Star Trek: Voyager debuted in 1995 as *The Next Generation* was ending. Its crew is immediately stranded in the far-off Delta Quadrant and faces a 75-year journey to return home. Not only are our new heroes not the center of

When *Voyager* debuted in 1995, the namesake ship was stranded far from the Federation and helmed by female captain Kathryn Janeway.

the universe, they can't even see Earth. And, perhaps not coincidentally, the leader of this lost ship is *Star Trek*'s first female captain, Kathryn Janeway (Kate Mulgrew). Even in the '90s, putting a woman at the lead of this iconic franchise was risky. Taylor, who helped create *Voyager* with producer and writer Rick Berman, says making her plausible wasn't easy.

"You have to assume that your captain can take care of things and is going to make the right decisions," Taylor says. "On the other hand, we didn't want to make her a man with breasts. I felt very strongly that there is a female sensibility and that that could be incorporated into this character without damaging her position. She could be intuitive, compassionate and feeling as well as having all the steely strength that she needed." Sometimes it came down to Mulgrew's hairstyle. "If it's too severe, then she loses her humanity. If it's too glamorous, she won't be taken seriously as a captain," says Taylor. Get it wrong, and fans would show their displeasure. It hasn't escaped Taylor's notice

The cast of *Enterprise* poses for a promotional shot. The most recent incarnation of the *Star Trek* franchise premiered just weeks after the 9/11 attacks.

that 20 years after Janeway took the bridge, female leaders are seen still trying to walk that line. (Just ask Hillary Clinton.)

Janeway is trying to get her crew home, not save the world. But *Voyager* often shows her as nostalgic for the days when this new frontier was like the Wild West. "Space must have seemed a whole lot bigger back then," she says of the original *Enterprise*. "It's not surprising they had to bend the rules a little. They were a little slower to invoke the Prime Directive and a little quicker to pull their phasers," she says. "But I have to admit, I would have loved to ride shotgun at least once with a group of officers like that."

Enterprise, a prequel set about 100 years before Kirk and Spock's time, was the first *Star Trek* series produced after the attacks of 9/11. A new American ethos of defending the homeland at all costs is threaded throughout the show. In the third season, Earth is attacked by a terrorist group and 7 million people are killed. The *Enterprise* is retrofitted as a military vessel so it can protect the planet.

That's not the only thing that was retro about *Enterprise*. While Voyager put women on the bridge, *Enterprise* put them back in bikinis. In "Bound," Capt. Jonathan Archer (Scott Bakula) receives a gift of beautiful green Orion slaves who mesmerize the male members of the crew with seductive dances. It is later discovered that the women emit hormones that make the men weak. Eventually, the crew concludes that it's really the men of Orion who are the slaves, not the women. "It's really the worst situation of victim blaming and stereotyping," says Timothy Sandefur. And given how sexual politics have changed even in the past 10 years, if this had first aired today, the producers would have been flooded with social-media outrage.

There hasn't been a *Star Trek* series since *Enterprise* ended in 2005. But CBS is cooking up a new one for 2017. And it won't be surprising if the creators try to revive some of the spirit of the original series. Those old-school heroics and all that moral certainty might be just the perfect balm for our new age of angst.

Susanna Schrobsdorff is assistant managing editor at TIME.

Which Captain Are You?

TIME's handy guide will help you find the bridge where you belong

BY SKYE GURNEY

Start here!

HOW DO YOU FEEL ABOUT HAVING YOUR MOLECULES REARRANGED?

IT'S NOT REALLY MY THING

BEAM ME UP, SCOTTY!

DO YOU ENJOY WORKING CLOSELY WITH VULCANS?

CAN'T LIVE WITHOUT THEM

I'D PREFER AN ANDROID OR A TRILL INSTEAD

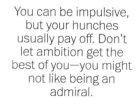

YOU MIGHT NOT BE CUT OUT FOR STARFLEET MANAGEMENT

Report to Lt. Barclay for career counseling.

WILL YOU BE KEEPING A PET ABOARD THE SHIP?

WHAT DO YOU DRINK TO STAY SHARP ON THE BRIDGE?

NO

YES

TEA. EARL GREY. HOT.

A STRONG KLINGON COFFEE

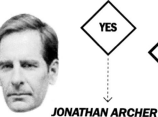

JONATHAN ARCHER

Even though you'll need to learn on the job, leadership comes naturally to you. Don't give up on that "Federation" idea—you never know what the future will bring!

BENJAMIN SISKO

You're a brilliant tactician (and baseball coach!). We promise the Orb of Prophecy has something interesting in store for you.

HOW SERIOUSLY DO YOU TAKE THE PRIME DIRECTIVE?

IT'S KIND OF A CASE-BY-CASE THING FOR ME

I WOULD STRAND MY CREW A QUADRANT AWAY

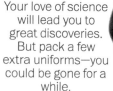

JAMES T. KIRK

You can be impulsive, but your hunches usually pay off. Don't let ambition get the best of you—you might not like being an admiral.

KATHRYN JANEWAY

Your love of science will lead you to great discoveries. But pack a few extra uniforms—you could be gone for a while.

JEAN-LUC PICARD

You have the heart of an explorer (even if it's artificial). A natural diplomat, you are surprisingly patient with cranky Klingons. Just try to stay away from the Borg!

TIME

Editor Nancy Gibbs
Creative Director D.W. Pine
Director of Photography Kira Pollack

STAR TREK
INSIDE THE MOST INFLUENTIAL SCIENCE-FICTION SERIES EVER

Editor Thomas E. Weber
Designer Skye Gurney
Photo Editor C. Tiffany Lee-Ramos
Writers Eliana Dockterman, Alex Fitzpatrick, Jeffrey Kluger, Courtney Mifsud, Susanna Schrobsdorff, William Shatner, Reed Tucker, Justin Worland, Richard Zoglin
Copy Editor Joseph McCombs
Reporter Andréa Ford
Editorial Production David Sloan

TIME INC. BOOKS
Publisher Margot Schupf
Associate Publisher Allison Devlin
Vice President, Finance Terri Lombardi
Vice President, Marketing Jeremy Biloon
Executive Director, Marketing Services Carol Pittard
Director, Brand Marketing Jean Kennedy
Finance Director Kevin Harrington
Assistant General Counsel Andrew Goldberg
Assistant Director, Production Susan Chodakiewicz
Senior Manager, Category Marketing Bryan Christian
Brand Manager Katherine Barnet
Associate Prepress Manager Alex Voznesenskiy
Project Manager Hillary Leary

Editorial Director Kostya Kennedy
Creative Director Gary Stewart
Director of Photography Christina Lieberman
Editorial Operations Director Jamie Roth Major
Senior Editor Alyssa Smith
Assistant Art Director Anne-Michelle Gallero
Copy Chief Rina Bander
Assistant Managing Editor Gina Scauzillo
Assistant Editor Courtney Mifsud

Special thanks: Don Armstrong, Brad Beatson, Nicole Fisher, Kristina Jutzi, Seniqua Koger, Kate Roncinske

Copyright © 2016 Time Inc. Books
Published by Time Books, an imprint of Time Inc. Books
225 Liberty Street · New York, NY 10281

Credits

GALACTIC WISDOM

"LEAVE ANY BIGOTRY IN YOUR QUARTERS. THERE'S NO ROOM FOR IT ON THE BRIDGE."

—*KIRK, "BALANCE OF TERROR"*

"Lying is a skill like any other. And if you want to maintain a level of excellence, you have to practice constantly."

—*GARAK, "IN PURGA-TORY'S SHADOW"*

"I CHOSE TO BELIEVE THAT I WAS A PERSON, THAT I HAD THE POTENTIAL TO BE MORE THAN A COLLECTION OF CIRCUITS AND SUB-PROCESSORS."

—*DATA, "RIGHTFUL HEIR"*

"WITHOUT FOLLOWERS, EVIL CANNOT SPREAD."

—*SPOCK, "AND THE CHILDREN SHALL LEAD"*

"YOU DON'T GRAB POWER. YOU ACCUMULATE IT QUIETLY, WITHOUT ANYONE NOTICING."

—*ZEK, "THE NAGUS"*

"I am pleased to see that we have differences. May we together become greater than the sum of both of us."

—*SURAK OF VULCAN, "THE SAVAGE CURTAIN"*

"Fear exists for one purpose: to be conquered."

—*JANEWAY, "THE THAW"*

"Seize the time, Meribor. Live now; make now always the most precious time. Now will never come again."

—*PICARD, "THE INNER LIGHT"*

"TOO MANY PEOPLE DREAM OF PLACES THEY'LL NEVER GO, WISH FOR THINGS THEY'LL NEVER HAVE, INSTEAD OF PAYING ADEQUATE ATTENTION TO THEIR REAL LIVES."

—*ODO, "IF WISHES WERE HORSES"*